KEYNES AND SCHUMPETER: NEW PERSPECTIVES

For Nalini

Keynes and Schumpeter:
New Perspectives

CHAITRAM J. TALELE

Department of Economics
Columbia State Community College

Avebury

Aldershot · Brookfield USA · Hong Kong · Singapore · Sydney

Published by
Avebury
Academic Publishing Group
Gower House
Croft Road
Aldershot
Hants
GU11 3HR

Gower Publishing Company
Old Post Road
Brookfield
Vermont 05036
USA

A CIP catalogue record for this book is available from the British Library and the US Library of Congress.

ISBN 1 85628 181 7

Printed in Great Britain by Athenaeum Press Ltd, Newcastle upon Tyne.

Contents

Introduction   vii

1   Essence of the Classical and Neoclassical Theories
of Interest   1

2   Theories of Interest—Keynes and Schumpeter   5

3   Treatment of Uncertainty and Entrepreneurial Function—
Keynes and Schumpeter   26

4   Integration of Money—Keynes and Schumpeter   35

5   The Role of Imperfect Competition—
Keynes and Schumpeter   46

6   Application of Stigler's Criteria—
Keynes and Schumpeter   56

7   The Future—Keynes and Schumpeter   60

8   Keynes's Theory of Probability and Induction   82

9   Viability of Keynesian Economics   107

10   The Age of Schumpeter   129

Preface

I would like to express my gratitude to Veronica Goodloe for her promptness, patience and understanding. Without her technical expertise this book would not have been completed. My daughter, Anjali, and son, Amitabh, have been a constant source of encouragement in completing this enterprise of writing a book. I am thankful to them for standing by and the encouragment they gave. Thanks are also due to Dr. L. Paul Sands, President, and Dr. William Muehlbauer, Dean of Administrative Services, both of Columbia State Community College.

Introduction

An interesting fact about Keynes and Schumpeter, the two greatest economists of the first half of the twentieth century, is that both thought rate of interest to be a monetary phenomena. Differences between them are wide and unbridgeable. Interestingly enough there are remarkable similarities, which have gone unnoticed and unstudied, between them concerning their views on Ricardian monetary theory, theory of rate of interest, role of imperfect competition and entrepreneurial function. The major focus of this study is on their theories of rate of interest. The discussion of their theories of interest inevitably involves the discussion of monetary theory in general, role of imperfect competition and the entrepreneurial function. The two quotations given below strike the note of the discussion that follows.

Schumpeter realizes the fact that Keynes, like him, brought back the idea of interest being mainly a monetary phenomena. It should be noted here that Schumpeter does not subscribe to Keynes's theory of rate of interest (1951, 1965, p. 286). Schumpeter expresses it in the following way.

And we were made to sit up to some purpose. For many more of us will now listen to the proposition that interest is a purely monetary phenomenon than we were ready to listen thirty-five years ago.

Next quotation comes from Edmond Malinvaud's classic article, "Capital Accumulation and Efficient Allocation of Resources." After discussing rigorously the rate of interest as a part of the price system in a purely competitive non-monetary economy in the above article, Malinvaud (1969, p. 679) expresses a lurking doubt concerning the rate of interest in the way given below.

One may wonder, moreover, whether it has always been realized that interest rates to be associated with chronics do not exist independently of the monetary conditions ruling the economy.

As pointed out earlier, the two quotations above set the tone and provide the background for the forthcoming discussion. It should be pointed out here that it is not the author's intention to prove or to disprove whether the rate of interest is purely a monetary phenomenon. The author's interest steams from the fact the two of the greatest minds in economics should think that way. Besides, determination of interest is but a part of of the problem. Other inseparable issues of the monetary theory, imperfect competition and entrepreneurial function are involved.

The plan of discussion is as follows. First, the true essence of the classical and neoclassical theory is given. It is not discussed in great details because such a discussion can be found in any standard work on interest. The author fully realizes that there are differences among the classical and neoclassical economists regarding the nature and determination of interest, but there is an accepted body of knowledge that is generally referred to as the neoclassical theory of interest. Second, Schumpeterian and Keynesian theories of interest are stated. Third, above theories are compared and contrasted from the point of view of the monetary theory, imperfect competition and entrepreneurial function.

1 Essence of the classical and neoclassical theories of interest

Adam Smith, a classical economist, emphasized parsimony as one of the important factors in propelling economic growth. Adam Smith (1716, 1937 Edition, p. 321) has expressed the idea in the following way.

Capitals are increased by parsimony and diminished by prodigibity and misconduct. Whatever a person saves from his revenue he adds to his capital, and either employs it himself in maintaining an additional number of productive hands, or enables some other person to do so by lending it to him for interest, that is, for a share of the profits. As the capital of an individual can be increased only by what he saves from his annual revenue or his annual gains, so the capital of a society, which is the same with that of all individuals who compose it, can be increased in the same manner.

Similar ideas are echoed through the works of other economists to this very day, although not without qualification. By foregoing present consumption—that is by saving—an individual can purchase productive resources so that his future income is augmented and consequently, standard of living is increased. For a society to form capital and wealth, capital goods must be produced, and resources must be diverted from the production of consumer's goods to the production of capital goods. Thus, in aggregate sense, society must forego present consumption for capital formation. But process of saving in reality is more complex than hypothesized by the classicists.

Thrift alone does not conjure the desired result. Productivity must accompany parsimony. It was left to Eugen Von Bohm-Bawerk to bring into play the concepts of period of production and roundaboutness in the production process. In his *Capital and Interest* Bohm-Bawerk has given an appropriate illustration to clinch his point on the above matter. If one were living alone in a cabin by a lake, one could walk by every time one needs water. Or, one could expend time and effort to construct a bucket to save the trip and have substantial amounts of water on hand whenever needed. Or, one could devote even more time and labor and construct a trough from a spring, running it past the cabin door to have the water readily available whenever it is needed. Thus, water for consumption can be obtained directly or in a roundabout way. Deployment of the roundabout method assures greater quantity of water for consumption, with a given amount of effort, compared to the cumbersome direct method. Hence the moral of the story is that more roundaboutness in production of capital goods created increased productivity, output per man-hour and higher standard of living. The neoclassical theory of interest advances the classical theory in the sense that it adds to the later conceptual and theoretical developments put forward by the later economists. The neoclassical theory allows the freedom of choice to save or dissave to individuals. Those who prefer to save today are said to have a preference for the future consumption over the present consumption. Through the financial intermediation, business will invest the savings for which it will yield higher real output in the future. From the yield on investment, the business pays interest to savers. According to the neoclassical theory, the positively sloping supply of saving is based on time preference and the negatively sloping demand for investment is nothing but the value of the marginal product of capital. Through the interaction of demand and supply the equilibrium rate of interest creates equality of saving and investment. In view of the neoclassical economists, the rate of interest is the price that rations the available supply of saving to borrowers and induces suppliers of saving to enter the market. In the neoclassical system it is recognized that volume of saving depends both on the interest rate and the level of income. It is the productivity of real capital assets which serves as the basis of demand for investable funds and the real rate of interest is the rate of return on capital assets. The money rate of interest charged on loanable funds represents the reflection of the real rate of interest determined by time-preference and productivity of capital.

To tighten the discussion analytically certain implicit assumptions underlying need to be clarified. The discussion of interest in the neoclassical theory is predicated on the assumption of an economy in which monetary unit only serves as a unit of account. For practical purposes the economy is assumed to be a barter economy. Also the saving investment process is complete and frictionless. In addition to the above, it is assumed that capital market is perfectly competitive and works in an environment of perfect certainty.

As pointed out earlier the demand for capital is based on the (marginal) productivity of capital. The logic behind this is that the prospective yields from an investment project are in excess of the total costs of funding the project. Let N represent life expectancy of a project in years and P_1, P_2..... $+ P_n$ be the prospective stream of net returns. The sum of $P_1 + P_2... + P_n$ must exceed T, the total cost of plant and equipment. The marginal productivity of capital is the rate that equalizes the present value of the stream of prospective yields with cost of plant and equipment. The rate, h, is the one which satisfies the following equation.

$$\frac{P_1}{1 + h} + \frac{P_2}{(1 + h)^2} + \cdots + \frac{P_n}{(1 + h)^n} - T = O$$

In the neoclassical world of perfect capital market and certainty, investment will be undertaken till marginal rate of return, h, exceeds or equals the rate of interest, r. On the other hand, investors will not undertake investment whose rate of return is less than r. In this situation, as can be seen, the rate of interest serves as an instrument of rationing the allocation of scarce capital funds among the competing investment project in an optimum way. From the above analysis it can be inferred that at a lower rate of interest more investment projects will be undertaken. This amounts to saying that investment demand curve slopes negatively, that is, at lower rate of interest more investment will be carried out and vice versa. This analytic is depicted in Figure 1.1.

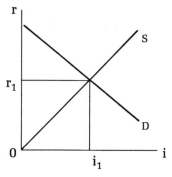

Figure 1.1

3

The vertical axis represents the real rate of interest r, and the horizontal axis represents the magnitude of investment, i. D is the negatively sloping demand curve for investment. The positively sloping supply curve, S, represents the supply of savings or loans. The saver is in an optimum position, in the case of two-period horizon when his marginal rate of substitution of future consumption and present consumption with $1 + r$ is equalized. For a person with n period horizon, $C_2, C_3, ..., C_n$ be the planned stream of future consumption and let C_T be the consumption of initial period t. The planned stream of future consumption can be considered as a single composite commodity C_F, which is equal to the constant level of consumption each period in future having the same present value as $C_2, C_3, ...C_n$. It can be symbolized in the following way.

$$\sum_{t=2}^{n} \frac{C_F}{(1+r)\,t-1} = C_F \sum_{t=2}^{n} \frac{1}{(1+r)\,t-1} = \sum_{t=2}^{n} \frac{C_T}{(1+r)\,t-1}$$

It can be proven that the optimum marginal rate of substitution of future (C^F) for present (C_T) consumption in the above situation is:

$$\frac{r}{1 - \left(\dfrac{1}{1+r}\right) n - 1}$$

It implies that the person in his optimum position can be persuaded to forego a dollar of consumption by rewarding him a constant stream of future consumption of r dollars. On the positively sloping supply curve, S, in Figure 1.1, in relation to any additional magnitude of investment undertaken, any r equals the marginal time preference of the community. The equilibrium rate of interest simultaneously represents the marginal productivity of capital and the marginal rate of substitution between future and present consumption.

2 Theories of interest – Keynes and Schumpeter

Lloyd Metzler (1951, pp. 93-116) realized the similarity between Keynes and Schumpeter concerning the monetary theory of rate of interest. In discussing the impact of the real balance effect, advocated by Pigou, on the theory of the rate of interest, Metzler makes the following point.

In this respect Pigou, the archdefender of classical economics, has deserted Mill and Marshall and joined Schumpeter and Keynes.

Both Keynes and Schumpeter believe that time preference and productivity of capital are not the factors that determine the rate of interest. According to Keynes it is impossible to deduce the rate of interest merely from time preference and the demand for investment. In his view there are two aspects to what he calls the psychological time preferences of an individual which involve two sets of decisions on the part of the individual. The first aspect of time preference of an individual is concerned with the individual consumption function, i.e., how much of income an individual will consume and how much he will save in some form to have a command over future consumption. As can be seen, so far, there is no difference between Keynes and the neoclassicists. But it is exactly at this point in his analysis Keynes sows the seeds of his monetary theory of interest. In the neoclassical system the individual makes the appropriate decision on the margin concerning future versus present consumption and his savings are turned into investment through the intermediation of financial institutions. At this point Keynes advances economic analysis by looking into the form in which individual decides to hold his saving. Unlike the neoclassical theory, the process for the individual does not end automatically after the act of saving. The individual confronts a genuine economic decision concerning the form in which he would prefer, given the market conditions, to hold his saving. Keynes (1936, p. 166) appropriately expresses this.

> But this decision having been made, there is a further decision which awaits him, namely, in what form he will hold the command over future consumption which he has reserved, whether out of his current income or from previous savings. Does he want to hold it in the form of immediate, liquid command (i.e. money or its equivalent)? Or is he prepared to part with immediate command for a specified or indefinite period, leaving it to future market conditions to determine on what terms he can, if necessary, convert deferred command over specific goods in general? In other words, what is the degree of liquidity-preference where an individual's liquidity-preference is given by a schedule of amounts of his resources, valued in terms of money or of wage-units, which he will wish to retain in the form of money in different sets of circumstances?

To Keynes the act of saving, as important as it is, is not the crucial factor in determining the rate of interest. A person could go on saving without ever lending it. That is the reason why interest cannot be a return for savings or waiting. The act that must follow concerns the person's liquidity preference. The choice confronted by the individual is either to have cash or trade the cash for somebody's debt. Keynes (1936, p. 167) emphatically attempts to point out the monetary nature of the rate of interest.

> On the contrary, the mere definition of the rate of interest tells us in so many words that the rate of interest is the reward for parting with liquidity for a specified period. For the rate of interest is, in itself, nothing more that the inverse proportion between a sum of money and what can be obtained for parting with control over money in exchange for a debt for a stated period of time.

Certain implications follow from Keynes's view. First, he emphasizes the role of money as a store of value which is unlike the previous theories. Second, since the rate of interest is a monetary phenomenon, does it not exist in a barter economy? In previous theories the discussion of the determination of the rate of interest is carried on only in real terms. Fisher (1930 and 1977, p. 43) clearly states this.

In the Keynesian system, the liquidity preference, that is, demand for money and quantity of money, that is, supply of money through their interaction determine the rate of interest. Keynes (1936, p. 167) brings the two factors together in the following way.

> If this explanation is correct, the quantity of money is the other factor which, in conjunction with liquidity preference, determine the actual rate of interest in given circumstances.

In figure 2.1 the simple Keynesian equilibrium is depicted. On the vertical axis, r represents the rate of interest. On the horizontal axis MS represents the money supply, LP curve represents the liquidity preference.

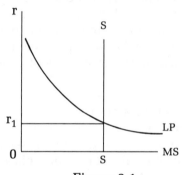

Figure 2.1

The reason for the existence of liquidity preference is uncertainty, particularly, uncertainty concerning the future rate of interest. Keynes holds an unusual subjective view, which is based upon the theory of probability, concerning the calculation of probabilities. Keynes's theory of liquidity preference is embedded in his theory of probability. The statement by Keynes (1936, p. 169) fully reflects it.

> The actuarial profit or mathematical expectation of gain calculated in accordance with existing probabilities—if it can be so calculated, which is doubtful—must be sufficient to compensate for the risk of disappointment.

The forthcoming discussion deals with Schumpeter's theory of interest the starting point of which is the stationary state.

The use of stationary state as an initial analytical device or as a launching pad has not been uncommon in economics. Economists of high reputation such as Alfred Marshall and J.B. Clark have made use of it. Schumpeter also makes use of the stationary state as an analytical device and as a necessary prelude to his scheme of things. Schumpeter's use of the stationary state had created a controversy among economists of the stature of Lionel Robbins, Frank Knight and Paul Samuelson. Explanation of the complex economic reality in its entirety is not always possible and often not desirable. It is not always possible because too many variables are involved and to account for the interaction of all of them is unwieldy. It is not desirable because the exposition loses the most required attributes of an explanation—simplicity. Use of parables, anecdotes and other intellectual instruments serve the purpose effectively. Of course, it must be understood that these methods have their own limits, particularly in scientific explanation. The forthcoming discussion intends to deal adequately with Schumpeter's use of the stationary state. The following two quotations from Marshall and Blaugh support the point that Schumpeter was not alone in using this technique in his discourse on economic development.

Marshall (1903, p. 415) uses the concept of stationary state as an analytical device to investigate the properties of a general equilibrium system.

What I take to be a static state is... a position of rest due to the equivalence of opposing forces which tend to produce motion. I cannot conceive of any static state which resembles the real world closely enough to form a subject of profitable study, and which is set aside even for an instant.

According to Blaugh (1985, p. 519), J.B. Clark also employed the construct of the stationary state in his refutation of the time-dimension concept of capital of the Austrian school.

If we confine ourselves to stationary conditions, Clark argues, the length of time for which a stock of capital is embodied in production turns out to be economically irrelevant. In stationary equilibrium, with not investment equal to zero the the number of production periods that are coming to a close at any instant of time are exactly equal to the number of production periods just beginning.

A careful discernment indicates that both Marshall and Clark are using the concept of the stationary state that suits their purposes at hand. Marshall's hypothetical system is at a position of rest and stable whereas Clark wants to refute the Austrian periods of production. The germane point of the discussion is the deployment of the concept to appropriately serve the purpose at hand.

Schumpeter's circular flow or stationary state is essentially characterized by the endless repetition of the same process of production and the fixity of all the relevant data, that is the supplies of productive resources and the acquired techniques. Schumpeter (1934, p. 36) states the essence of his circular flow in the following way.

We are not now speaking of the introduction of new processes, but of the circular flow which consists of given processes already in working order... Given the necessary quantities of labor and natural agents, production by this method will be repeated indefinitely without any exercise of choice, and the stream of products will be continuous. But even if that were not the case, there would be no underestimation of future products. For if productive process turned out its results in periodic intervals there would still be no waiting, because consumption adapt itself and run on continuously and at an equal rate per unit of time, so that there would be no motive for underestimating future products.

Schumpeter raises an interesting question and answers it himself. The question Schumpeter raises boils down to saying that in this hypothetical world of a zero rate of interest would not consumers dissave? That is, since the rate of interest is zero, people will start consuming the available capital which will eventually lead to the decrease in total amount of capital. To fix the idea of interest in general and in Schumpeterian sense in particular, a graphic presentation could be borrowed fruitfully from Ramsey's mathematical theory of saving. Ramsey (1928, pp. 543-59) has propounded an elegant theory of the determination of the rate of interest according to which the rate of interest at any given time may be determined directly from the interaction of existing quantity of capital in society and the marginal productivity of investment which this quantity determines.

Figure 2.2 is directly borrowed from Ramsey. In it a demand curve represents the quantity of capital in relation to the rate of return it will yield. In mathematical terms it denotes the partial derivative of income with respect to capital. A vertical line C represents the existing amount of capital, and its intersection with the demand curves shows the rate of interest. Vertical axis represent the rate of interest in percentage terms. Horizontal axis represents the magnitude of capital. A horizontal line i is depicted at a level showing the rate at which all persons in the community, at present and in the future, dis-

9

count future utilities. Because the rate of interest r is higher than i in this illustration, abstinence occurs. In other words net saving is positive. According to Ramsey, the rate of saving and investment will depend roughly on the ratio BD/AC, that is the ratio of i to r.

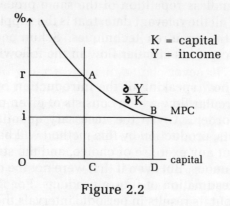

Figure 2.2

As can be seen, in the Ramsey model the existing stock of capital determines the rate of interest without reference to time preference or the rate of investment. In absence of innovation and technological change, rate of investment would determine the gradual descent of the demand curve over time.

The same diagram could be utilized to indicate the Schumpeterian situation concerning capital in a circular flow.

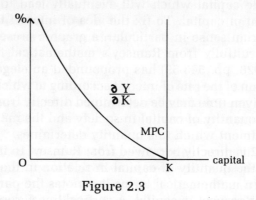

Figure 2.3

In Figure 2.3, as in the previous diagram, the existing stock of capital determines the rate of interest, which is zero, without reference to time preference or the rate of investment. The rate of net investment is also zero. Since both i and r are zero, no abstinence occurs. Net

10

saving in this situation is zero. These are the results Schumpeter wants to convey from his circular flow.

From the total perspective of Schumpeterian economics, it would be reasonable to state that he wants to explain the dynamic essence of the capitalistic system which according to him is entirely due to entrepreneur and his innovations. The prelude of the circular flow is simply to serve as a frame of reference and the idea of a zero rate of interest in such a state also has a purpose in that context only according to Schumpeter. He never claims that the circular flow has a correspondence with reality today or with any historic time. Nevertheless, the idea of a zero rate of interest in the particular context of the stationary state has become very controversial. Samuelson (1966, p. 205) neatly sums up the context and reason for such a debate.

For a question of fact is not being debated, but rather a question of logical possibility and necessity emerging a particular set agreed-upon axioms.

Professor Lionel Robbins (1930, pp. 194-214) has leveled the following criticism upon Schumpeter's notion of a zero rate of interest in a stationary economy. According to Robbins under the conditions of a zero rate of interest there is no reason for the individuals and community to replenish the depreciated capital to keep it up to the par for the continuance of the production. By the definition of the stationary state, there is no technological change but for the given production to continue the depreciated capital must be replenished. Since the rate of interest is zero there is no incentive to devote resources for such a replenishment in Robbins's view. Robbins states his view in the following way.

Why should labour and the use of material factors be devoted to the maintenance of the produced means of production if no net remuneration is forthcoming?

Robbins advances his argument further by stating that not only will people not replenish the depreciated capital but they also will not refrain from consuming it. They will start eating part by part a goose that lays golden eggs. According to Robbins, if there is no yield on the use of capital assets, the assets themselves would be eaten away. His views are given below.

For if there is no yield to the use of capital (no reinertrag), there would be no reason to refrain from consuming it... It is in short an

11

interest rate, which, other things being given, keeps the stationary state stationary—the rate at which it does not pay to turn income into capital or capital into income.

Professor Samuelson offers a valiant defense of his teacher. Samuelson's arguments are clearly stated and are in accordance with the logic of economic theory. He states that in economic theory individuals and entrepreneurs are assumed to be rational. The setting of the stationary state is composed of the world of perfect certainty and perfect competition. In such a situation of perfect foresight, rational individuals will refrain from eating up their capital at a zero rate of interest. Because of their perfect foresight individuals will realize that not replenishing of the depreciated capital will progressively diminish their material standard of living.

According to Samuelson, a given income has certain utility which leads to maximization. Once used to that level of utility maximization, people will try to maintain the capital (not eat it up) to procure the level of total utility they are used to. He (Samuelson, 1966, p. 205) puts his argument in a clear way.

> For our purposes it is convenient to adopt the quite arbitrary assumption that utility is a given function of income in each period; more specifically, that it is the same function at each instant of time and that the individual acts so as to maximize the sum of utilities thus defined over all future time.

In Samuelson's view this is the logic of the argument that Schumpeter has in mind. Samuelson's argument can also be supported and firmed up by the evidence of the present studies of aggregate consumption. The asymmetrical behavior of consumers is well known. In aggregate consumers are always willing and eager to increase their consumption whenever income increases but are not willing to lower their consumption when income decreases. On this factual basis it can be argued that in a world of perfect certainty and foresight consumers will not fail to replenish their capital, which if they do not, will lower their standard of living. People will realize that to get golden eggs from a goose, the goose has to be kept alive and cared for. Eating it up in parts for the present delight spells trouble. Their perfect foresight will make them realize the danger of doing that.

Samuelson also considers and refutes the possibility of people saving today for capital formation in anticipating of the future higher income than what they have presently in a stationary economy. Samuelson eliminates this possibility on the grounds that anticipated additions of marginal utilities of the future will be smaller because they are predicated on the basis of today's smaller income. On the grounds of marginal utility theory, diminishing marginal utility would not allow people to subtract from the present income because the subtractions from present income would result in greater losses of utility due to the smallness of present income. If the rate of interest is zero and there is no time preference, even distribution of income over time yields an optimal solution. The argument leads to the conclusion that under such circumstances there will be no accumulation or decumulation of capital.

Because this constitutes the gist of Samuelson's refutation of Robbins's argument, it would be appropriate to quote Samuelson (1966, p. 63) here.

> For the increment of future consumption would add marginal units of utility which are lower simply because they are superimposed upon existing income. On the other hand, because of diminishing utility, the subtractions from present income would result in greater losses of utility because of the smallness of present income. Only an even distribution of income over time is optimal if the rate of interest is zero, and if there is no time preference. This means there is no decumulation of capital, and a similar argument shows that there would be no accumulation.

The second point of controversy concerning Schumpeter's stationary state centers around the lack of abstinence. This point of criticism needs to be sorted out carefully. First, the dominant role that abstinence plays in the interest theories of Bohm-Bawerk and Fisher is totally relegated to minor importance, if at all, in Schumpeter's theory of interest. Second, according to Schumpeter, in a stationary state since there is no accumulation and decumulation, as discussed above, there is no need for abstinence. It is the second point on which the discussion is centered here. Schumpeter is aware of the seriousness of the problem. Schumpeter (1934, p. 37) is frank enough to admit the seriousness of the problem and states that its existence cannot be denied. In his view the process of abstinence and capital formation is much more complicated than it has the appearance of but has not yet been dealt with the penetrating analysis that it deserves to be dealt with. Careful reading of Schumpeter reveals that he makes a clear distinction between the process of creating a productive apparatus and that of operating it once it is created. It is the latter with which he is concerned as far as his treatment of the stationary state is concerned.

Schumpeter's answer can be systematically analyzed. According to him by assumption there are only two factors of production that receive income and they are labor and land. As shown in Figure 2.3 OK is the amount of capital on which the rate of interest is zero. Schumpeter also denies the possibility of interest charges lingering on the capital previously accumulated because according to him abstinence is not the reason for the existence of the rate of interest. It only plays a secondary role in the supply of capital. In a dynamic sense when innovations occur the introduction of new methods of production does not require previous capital. Abstinence, particularly in the circular flow, is not an element of economic process because he envisages the circular flow, after its establishment, to be continuous unbroken process. He does not think that saving, investment, and capital formation as discrete and intermittently broken events. He (1930, p. 38) depicts it in the way given below.

> Whatever may the nature of waiting, it certainly is not an element of economic process which we are here considering, because the circular flow, once established, leaves no gaps between outlay and productive effort and satisfaction of wants. Both are, following professor Clark's conclusive expression, automatically synchronized.

As far as the synchronization aspect of Schumpeter's argument is concerned, Samuelson thinks it could be best justified by appealing to the logic of balancing marginal utilities, as discussed previously, in the events of accumulation and decumulation. But repeated reading of this part of Schumpeter imprints on one's mind that the main thrust of his argument is directed towards denying the prime role to the notion of abstinence or time preference which inevitably involves the calculus of marginal utilities. The tenor of his argument leaves the impression that Schumpeter's stationary state is so well set, smooth, frictionless and continuous in its operation that things Schumpeter wants to happen happen despite the acting agents in that system. Besides, it cannot be forgotten that Schumpeter has a purpose in mind in setting up the things he has done. And the purpose is to contrast this stationary state with his dynamics.

Frank Knight has objected to Schumpeter's idea of a zero rate of interest from the point of view of demand. Knight (1956, p. 191) states his idea with reference to the basic economic logic.

> It seems to the writer that under any realistic conditions as to wants and conditions of supply, goods requiring a longer time to

produce must have greater value for the same expenditure of ultimate resource-services other than time. The supply of "time" in production is limited by the supply of consumable goods in general, and it must command a price unless all goods are free and the conditions of economic life consequently non-existent.

Knight's objection to Schumpeter is narrowly and carefully focused. Above objection to Schumpeter apart, Knight concurs with Schumpeter in denying a prime role to time preference in the determination of interest. Furthermore, Knight suggests an amendment in Schumpeter's argument to make it what he calls "realistic" by suggesting that in a stationary state interest rate should be adequate enough to prevent consumption of existing capital without inducing further addition to it. In a way Knight does not even object to the use of stationary state as such, in fact with approval he suggests something akin to Mill's stationary state, except the idea of a zero rate of interest is not palatable to him because it abnegates the very existence of the basic economic problem.

Samuelson answers Knight on the basis of mathematical reasoning reached by Ramsey the essence of which is that a rational maximizing individual would only find it optimal to increase his capital at a decreasing rate so as to approach a zero rate without ever reaching it. Another interesting criticism of Samuelson's defense of Schumpeter is given by Whitaker (Samuelson, 1979, p. 142). The essence of the criticism is that in the world of perfect competition consumers act independently of each other without affecting prices at all. In such a situation the implication is that some might save and others might dissave. Interesting possibilities are likely to emerge in this situation. On the average if savers balance the dissavers, the net result would be no accumulation and decumulation. If savers save more than dissavers dissave or savers save less than dissavers, it would constitute a violation of the stationary state. The best defense in this situation is that, as pointed out before, under perfect competition all players also possess perfect foresight. In a world of certainty, perfect foresight and rational players, it is more likely that there will be no net addition or subtraction to or from the capital stock.

Extensive and in depth discussion of Schumpeter's stationary state or circular flow is given for the reasons outlined below. First, it involves very important and intricate issues of topics such as capital theory. Second, economists of high standing such as Samuelson, Robbins and Knight are involved in the polemics. Third, disproportionately large amounts of valuable resources of the economists of very high caliber have been expended on a topic that is simply a prelude to the magnificent dynamics of Schumpeter. Fourth, it also serves as proof of Schumpeter's analytical vision, depth and breadth of his rarely matched scholarship. He has expressed this (1964, p. 19) in his *Business Cycles*.

For our system is logically self-contained only if this is the case: we can be sure that we understand the nature of economic phenomena only if it is possible to deduce prices and quantities from the data by means of those relations and to prove that no other set of prices and physical quantities is compatible with both the data and the relations. The proof that this is so is the magna charta of economic theory as an autonomous science, assuring us that its subject matter is a cosmos and not a chaos. It is the rationale of the idea of variables that do not vary, the justification of the schema of a stationary economic process.

The purpose Schumpeter has in mind in using the stationary state is best explained by him in his *Business Cycles* by stating that the method is analogous to the method known in mechanics as the method of virtual displacements. In mechanics the displacement is "virtual" if it is not actually experienced but merely imagined in the course of an analysis. This apt analogy underscores the analytical value and role Schumpeter has assigned to stationary economy. Also, it is indicative of the fact that Schumpeter has delved to the very intellectual bottom from the variety of angles.

There are only two income shares in a stationary economy. One, wages which go to workers. Two, rent which goes to natural resources. Since the rate of interest is zero there is no remuneration to capital. But in a dynamic economy, after the economic evolution is in high gears due to the entrepreneurial innovations profit emerges as an income to entrepreneur and it is from these profits interest on capital is paid. In that sense Schumpeter regards interest as a tax on profit. In a dynamic economy, payment of interest as reward to capital presupposes profit.

Schumpeter is definitely right when he states that something akin to the stationary state has been present in the theorization of economists of all vintages and schools. In this respect Schumpeter gets a very strong support from John Hicks. According to Hicks in the explanation of significant historical process such as capitalistic growth model, a scholar has to compare and contrast what actually happened with would have happened had something been different. Hicks contends that it is impossible to explain in economics without the use of counterfactual model of an economy which must be in equilibrium, at least to begin with. Let Hicks (1983, p. 113) state his case in his own words.

We know that the actual experience was not an equilibrium experience; there were surprises, and unforeseen changes of course, but it is hardly possible that the hypothetical experience should not be an equilibrium experience, for it is under our control, so there can be no surprise in it.

Schumpeter's hypothetical stationary state is in a state of equilibrium and his purpose is exactly what Hicks has in mind. The purpose is to have a stylized theoretical construct that would be completely under control and would help the theoretical and analytical take-off.

But it would not be right to stop here because what Sir John Hick states in further analysis fits the Schumpeter's case to the T. As pointed out above according to Sir John it is justified, even necessary, to concoct hypothetical equilibrium states as an initial analytical device. He continues and states that getting stuck in tracts of statics must be avoided if analysis has to advance. Sir John (1983, p. 124) effectively makes his case.

It will be clear, from what I have said already, why in my view that cannot be granted. I have (I think) shown that, so far as hypothetical constructions are concerned, the economy, during the period (or year) must be supposed to be in equilibrium. We cannot manage it otherwise. But to go on from that to suppose that is has always been in equilibrium is quite a different matter. It is a 'relapse into statics', as I have called it another place, a relapse into timelessness. It must be avoided.

In Schumpeterian system, once the entrepreneur and his innovations appear on the horizon banks, initially, finance these innovations by credit creation and the system is involved in a process of creative destruction.

In the interest of completeness it would be interesting to compare Knut Wicksell's deployment of a stationary state with Schumpeter's. At the outset it must be pointed out that both the theorists (Wicksell and Schumpeter) have different purposes in mind in using such a state. Wicksell basically wants to amend and advance the analysis of capital theory of Bohm-Bawerk, Jevons and Walras. Schumpeter, directly a student of Bohm-Bawerk and the other Austrians, wants to steer clear of all the controversies of the capital theory. Schumpeter's main objective is to create a system of his own and use the stationary state essentially as a take-off ground. He has propounded a theory of interest that under no circumstances could have been palatable to his master Bohm-Bawerk and the other Austrians. Time preference and periods

17

of production, the very essence of the Austrian theory, are not at all the ingredients of which Schumpeter's theory is made of. Schumpeter's monetary theory of interest is discussed at length at the place in this work. Immediate purpose at hand is to compare the theoretical use of stationary state. Wicksell (1898, 1965, p. 126) visualizes it in the following way.

> Under stationary conditions-which as the simplest possible assumption, should serve as a starting-point in all economic discussions-these goods will not be actually produced at all, they will be merely maintained; but the labor which is applied to them can on each occasion be regarded as representing a new investment of capital.

In Schumpeterian stationary system capital goods are maintained too—as long as the stationariness last. In a perfectly synchronized system of Schumpeter the depreciation is routinely charged to national income but there is no creation of new capital and consequently the rate of interest is zero.

Wicksell categorizes capital into two branches. First, he calls fixed capital (rent-earning goods) which is invested over a long period in tangible machines. Second, he calls liquid real capital or working capital. Schumpeter makes no such distinction. Perfect synchronization of consumption, production and exchange according to Schumpeter requires no working capital. According to Wicksell in the stationary economy fixed capital goods are not produced, but are only maintained. Investment incurred in these goods is a matter of past time and no longer be under consideration. In Wicksell's view the net interest on this capital has the character of rent because repair and maintenance costs fall on the capitalists who are currently using these goods. Wicksell specifically imputes the cost to the capitalists whereas Schumpeter lets it be taken care of by the synchronization process. Interest as a payment does exist even in a stationary state in the Wisksellian system. Because Schumpeter specifically wants to ascribe the emergence of interest to innovations, he is not willing to have it in a stationary state.

Upon reading Samuelson (1943, pp. 58-68) concerning this aspect of Schumpeter's work, one becomes aware of the debate aroused by the concept of the stationary state and its entailing phenomenon of the zero rate of interest. Samuelson ably defends Schumpeter's position, but at the same time points out that zero rate of interest is not absolutely necessary in obtaining the results Schumpeter desires and the stationary state in Schumpeter is nothing more than an expository device.

It is of crucial importance to realize analytically the significance of the circular flow in Schumpeter's view. He thought that it is impossible to bring out the fundamental facts in their simplest form without the model of the stationary state. Schumpeter firmly believes that the model of stationary state has been implicitly present in ratiocination of absolutely all economists of all the schools at all times.

Schumpeter emphatically rejects the notion of saving and accumulation on grounds that such a process presupposes previous profits that are used for the financing of innovations. This is contradictory in the Schumpeterian system because the stationary state is essentially characterized by the nonexistence of innovations. Innovating entrepreneurs borrow all the funds they require for implementing innovations. Nobody else borrows.

Schumpeter makes a clear distinction between normal credit and abnormal credit. Normal credit makes contribution to social dividend, what we today would call gross national product, in terms of existing goods and services. Abnormal credit, on the other hand, represents claims (certificates as Schumpeter calls them) to future services or to goods yet to be produced. According to Schumpeter, both normal and abnormal credit act as means of payment, but in practice are hard to distinguish.

Schumpeter does not rule out other kinds of credit-consumptive credit. But he thinks that is not an essential element in the process of economic development. In the circular flow, production is financed by current receipts. To prove his point, Schumpeter assumes that in the circular flow all the given (fixed) quantity of money consists of metal money with the given (constant) velocity circulation. In such a situation, given the conditions of the circular flow, there would be no need for credit. From this, Schumpeter infers that the essential element of the credit phenomenon is not to be found in the current credit within the circular flow.

After the production is over, the value of the output produced by the entrepreneur exceeds the value of the credit inflation. The non synchronous appearance of credit and commodities does create a semblance of inflation, but the excesses of goods produced actually creates deflation according to Schumpeter. Now the time has arrived for the entrepreneur to repay his debt. With the repayment of debts, the original bank credit disappears and the only remaining elements are entrepreneur's profit and interest. The repayment of debt sets in the deflationary process the size of which depends on the prolongation of certain enterprises in the process of competition. Schumpeter does see the possibility of lingering of the new purchasing power, which according to him (Schumpeter) would be of no avail because it would be covered by the goods produced and it might spur new enterprise (secondary wave by the imitators in the Schumpeterian sense).

After assigning so much importance to the process of credit creation in the entailing process of economic development, the most important consideration of which Schumpeter is well aware, is to investigate the limits of the process of credit creation. Schumpeter sets the following limits to this process. Schumpeter states that the banks, in order not to endanger their solvency, will give credit in such a way that the consequent inflation remains mild and is of short duration. Schumpeter (1934, p. 113) puts it effectively.

> And if the solvency of the banking system in this sense is not to be endangered, the banks can only give credit in such a way that the resulting inflation is really temporary and moreover remain moderate.

Should the inflation be higher and prolonged, according to Schumpeter, the banker siphons the purchasing power that was drawn from the circular flow as bank reserves to be kept by the central as well as the other banks. Of the total credit created, a small amount daily seeps into the trade. The smallness and the gradualness of the above process works the problem out according to Schumpeter. The adverse balance of payments created by inflation under the gold standard start an outflow of gold and could exacerbate the problem of insolvency. In Schumpeter's view this is not likely because the banks of all the countries expand credit more or less simultaneously. Here, Schumpeter is well aware of the tenuousness of his proposition. He states that no precise limits can be set to credit creation beforehand, and, in practice, might be determined by legislation and temperament of the people. Despite the limits, Schumpeter (1934, pp. 113-114) believes the significance of the process of credit creation cannot be belittled.

> Its (limit) existence neither excludes the creation of purchasing power in our sense nor alters its significance, but makes its volume at any time an elastic, though nevertheless of definite magnitude.

Capital, according to Schumpeter, does not consist of any concrete goods, but simply a device which enables the producer to divert the existing factors of production to their innovative use. He goes to a great length to distinguish between capital and other factors of production. An entrepreneur might have capital but not production goods. To Schumpeter, capital consists of a fund out of which productive services are paid for. This fund of purchasing power consists of money and other assets calculated in money. Schumpeter is aware of the fact that this way of defining capital somewhat resembles the definition of capital propounded by Menger and Fisher. But Schumpeter emphatically denies any more similarity than the minor initial one to the theories of Menger and Fisher. He (1934, p. 120) expresses his view in the following way.

However, this view, apparently so satisfactory at first sight, is unfortunately not completely adequate.

Schumpeter assigns the following functions to the money or capital market. The major function the money or capital market performs is to provide credit for the financing of economic development. This market is originated, evolved and nourished by the process of economic development. This market itself becomes a source of incomes. Schumpeter envisions the money/capital market as a nerve center or a computer brain of the capitalist system. All credit needs for the new projects are brought to this market; it compares and contrasts all the new projects. All kinds of wheeling and dealing and maneuvering goes in this market.

Schumpeter is willing to recognize the role of principle of time preference in the case of what he calls consumptive loan. In the case of productive loans (credit creation), in Schumpeterian system, the existence of interest presupposes the existence of profit. Profit as a remuneration to the innovative entrepreneurial services, to Schumpeter, is strictly a dynamic phenomenon. In a static economy or the Schumpeterian circular flow, profit does not exist. Since profit does not exist, interest cannot exist. The demand for credit originates from the financing of innovations by the new enterprises. The demand for credit that is supplied by the money market originates from the financing of innovations by the new enterprises. The old (non-innovating) business are routinely financed from the current return from their production. Here again, Schumpeter (1934, p. 158) has the following proposition which clearly indicates that he wanted to disassociate himself from the notion of the time preference.

From this, the rest follows—especially the theorem that interest attaches to money and not to goods.

It is extremely interesting to read Schumpeter dueling his master/teacher Bohm-Bawerk. Of the three reasons Bhom-Bawerk propounded for the existence of rate of interest, Schumpeter rejects one—namely, the discounting of the future enjoyments. Schumpeter rejects this because according to Schumpeter, Bohm-Bawerk asks us to accept it as a cause not itself requiring any explanation. As far as Bohm-Bawerk's first reason for the existence of rate of interest-changing relation between wants and means of satisfaction-is concerned, Schumpeter thinks it can be incorporated into his own theory of interest. Moreover, it is agreed upon by Wicksell and Mark Blaug (1962, p. 452) that the first reason of Bohm-Bawerk is concerned with the demand for consumption loans. Schumpeter clearly states that the demand for consumption loans does not figure at all in his theory of interest. Schumpeter thinks Bohm-Bawerk's third reason for interest (adoption of roundabout methods of production) could and should be construed as an entrepreneurial act. Upon doing so, it could be legitimately considered as one of the many subordinate cases Schumpeter's concept of carrying out new combinations. Repetition of the roundabout process of production, which gets incorporated into the circular flow, will not, in absence of innovation, generate net income according to Schumpeter.

According to Schumpeter, interest must be justified as a payment in capitalist society. Under the circular flow the total product must be imputed to the original factors of production that is to the services of labor and land. The competitive process of the circular flow annihilates any surplus of receipts over outlays. How can interest be, then, justified? Like Bohm-Bawerk, Schumpeter also rejects Senior's concept of abstinence. Bohm-Bawerk expresses it in the way given below.

It is (added) a logical blunder to represent the renunciation or postponement off gratification, or abstinence as a second independent sacrifice in addition to the labor sacrificed in production.

The above statement must not undermine Senior's contribution and the role of abstinence as a supply price in completion of the theory of interest. But according to Bohm-Bawerk and Schumpeter, the very nature of factor of production is such that abstinence cannot be recognized as an independent factor of production.

In Schumpeter's view, interest cannot be regarded as a return to the produced means of production. Schumpeter's reasoning in concern with this point is very Austrian. It runs in the following way. Produced means of production do produce more goods with higher values. The higher values of good will impart higher values to the produced means of production, which, in turn, will impute higher values to the original factors of production that help them produce. Consequently, no element of surplus value can be permanently imputed to intermediate means of production. In summary, in Schumpeter's view (1934, p. 163), as stated below, interest cannot be regarded as a permanent payment to the produced means of production.

Hence, on the basis of the arguments in first and fourth chapters and the reference to Bohm-Bawerk we can state that the above opens up no way out of the dilemma and no source of value at all exists here for the payment of interest.

According to Schumpeter, interest on productive loan exists because of the surplus created by economic development. Schumpeter divides the surplus values created by development into categories: (1) surplus value created by the more advantageous use than previously, and (2) surplus value created by the repercussions of development such as increase in actual or anticipated demand. Schumpeter regards interest as a value phenomenon and considers this to be the common element his theory shares with other theories of interest.

In Schumpeter's view, the problem of interest will be solved in economic theory when the permanent stream of interest flowing out always to the same capital from the transitory and ever-changing profit will be explained. Schumpeter thought that the classicists were successful in separating interest from the profit and also in recognizing that the source of interest was profit. But they were unsuccessful in proving why the creditor, owner of capital, is always successful in extracting his share of profit as interest and why the capital market always rewards him (creditor) that share. In the postmercantilist period, capital came to be associated with concrete goods which entrepreneur uses in production. Interest, then, was considered as an element in the price of concrete productive goods. Profits and interest were not properly delineated. Besides the unsatisfactory analysis of the entrepreneurial function contributed to the above practice.

In the process of economic development as a result of innovation, higher return on product could be obtained but the means of production which helped produce the product could be purchased at predevelopment (lower) prices. Consequently, the possibility of the emergence of profit will make the present sums of money to carry value premium which also will lead the price premium on products. This statement is the gist of Schumpeter's theory of interest.

Schumpeter's process of interest determination works through the interaction of demand for and supply of purchasing power in the following way. Demand originates from the entrepreneur. Entrepreneur is the one who values the present purchasing power over the future one. With credit creation element being actively involved, the supply of purchasing power comes from the banker. Possible limitations on the supply of credit in Schumpeter's view could come from two sources: (1) possible failure by the entrepreneur, and (2) possible depreciation of credit means of payment. Schumpeter thinks that first would be of no consequence because the banker charges premium in the rate of interest of the failure risk.

It would be highly appropriate to quote Schumpeter (1934, p. 190) on this subject.

> Only in the course of development is the matter different. Only then can I obtain a higher return for my product-that is if I carry out a new combination of the productive forces which I bought for hundred monetary units and succeed in putting a new product of higher values on the market. For the prices of the means of production were not determined with regard to this employment, but only with regard to previous uses. Here, then, the possession of a sum of money is the means of obtaining a bigger sum. On this account, and to this extent, a present sum will be normally valued more highly than a future sum. Therefore, the present sums of money—so to speak as potentially bigger sums—will have a value premium, which will also lead to a price premium. And in this lies the explanation of interest.

One successful innovation paves the way for other innovations swelling the demand for credit and making the rate of interest always positive. As the rate interest increases, some entrepreneurs are eliminated.

Schumpeter admits the possibility of accumulation of purchasing power during the pre-capitalist economy. But once the process of development is on its way, the following three sources of purchasing power materialize. First, entrepreneurial profits are ploughed back in substantial sums. Second, substantial sums also come from the earned profits of successful entrepreneurs/their heirs who are retired from active business. Third, the tempo of development does reward profit to some people other than entrepreneurs, of which to a greater or smaller extent flows to the money market.

In a developing economy, saving as such cannot be a large enough source of purchasing power because addition to saving sinks its marginal utility. Increase in the interest rate increases saving very little, if any, in this situation. An accessory stream of purchasing power flowing from the above source into money market is possible according to Schumpeter. An additional source of purchasing power could also be available from what Schumpeter terms the money which is idle for a longer or shorter time that could be lent upon the receipt of interest. These are the money balances held to meet an impending expenditure. By the use of highly developed technique, a banker is able to channel those funds into the supply of purchasing power.

All the sources discussed above augment the supply of purchasing power causing substantial reduction in the rate of interest. This spurs the process of economic development, but when economic development stagnates, the bankers hardly know what to do with the disposable funds. According to Schumpeter, this is indicative of the fact that: (1) interest is nothing more than the capital sum plus a premium for risk and compensation for labor, i.e., Schumpeter is denying the significance of time preference, and (2) the banker really is the creator and not simply a middleman between savers and investors. Schumpeter (1934, p. 201) expresses his view forcefully.

Whenever the development stagnates, the banker hardly knows what to do with the disposable funds, and often it becomes doubtful whether the price of money contains more than the capital sum plus a premium for risk and compensation for labor. Then especially, and particularly on the money markets of very rich nations, the element of creation of purchasing power often recedes into background, and the impression can easily be formed, so dear to the economic theory as well as the banking practice, that the banker is nothing more than a middleman between borrowers and lenders.

As can be discerned from the above passage, Schumpeter clearly thought of banks as more than merely middlemen between borrowers and lenders as the mainstream economic theory treats them.

3   Treatment of uncertainty and entrepreneurial function – Keynes and Schumpeter

Since a reference is made to the Keynes' theory of probability, some discussion of it is in order. To Keynes, probability is a logical relation which can be defined only in terms of rational belief. Rational belief is based on knowledge of the event. Our rational belief is P due to some proposition that h that we know of and also have the knowledge of p/h = a. Our premises must be based on p/h = a. From this it can be discerned that propositions concerning p/h = a must form the our syllogism. According to Keynes, there are two sources of knowledge: (1) part of our knowledge comes directly and (2) part by argument. Knowledge by argument springs from the direct knowledge of the form if p then q or q/p = a. In every syllogism from the major premise to conclusion inference must be based on the direct knowledge. In Keynes's view, rational belief of the appropriate degree exists because of the knowledge of h and of p/h = a. Keynes thinks that all direct knowledge is certain, and that rational belief which falls short of certainty can arise only through perception of a probability relation. Keynes (1973, pp. 15, 16) expresses it in the following way.

Knowledge, on the other hand, of a secondary proposition involving a degree of probability lower than certainty, together with knowledge of the premise of the secondary proposition, leads only to a rational belief of the appropriate degree in the primary proposition.

Keynes (1973, p. 16) states the relation between probability and certainty this way.

> Of probability we can say no more than it is a lower degree of rational belief than certainty; and we may say, if we like, it deals with degrees of certainty.

Except a very special class of probabilities, probabilities in general are not numerical according to Keynes. In his view one probability may not be comparable with another, that is, they may not be equal to, greater than or less than each other. He visualized probabilities in terms of the following geometrical form. There are two points of which 1 represents certainty at one end and the other represents impossibility at the other end. Numerically measurable probabilities could lie on the line between 0 and 1, while others could lie on curved routes from 0 to 1. Of the two probabilities lying on the same route, one closer to 1 can be said to be greater. But probabilities lying on different routes cannot be compared unless their routes intersect which is not altogether impossible.

The import of the extensive discussion of Keynes probability theory is that this ingrained view Keynes held has given strong tenor to the economics of Keynes. A careful discernment of his discussion of the general theory of interest reveals his lurking doubt about the numerical measurement of probabilities. Since objective numerical probability cannot be calculated, the recourse to the person involved in the situation is to have subjective probabilities. And on the basis of the subjective valuation certain amount of money will be demanded as an expression of his/her liquidity preference. The second factor Keynes brings to bear upon uncertainty and liquidity preference in an organized market is of swimming against the tide, so to say. If a person's opinion happens to be against the predominant majority, he might consider himself more vulnerable and enhance his liquidity preference.

Treatment of uncertainty has always been a very difficult problem in economics. Most of the time it is assumed away by assuming perfect competition. Solow's (1965, p. 15) remark below is characteristically witty and instructive in his regard.

> The fundamental difficulty of uncertainty cannot really be dodged, and since it cannot be faced, it must simply be ignored.

Problems that can be ignored in value theory cannot be in monetary theory, especially, in the case of Keynes, he made uncertainty as the reason for liquidity preference. Another important point in econometrics though not of immediate relevance is that Keynes steadfastly refused to endorse econometrics wholeheartedly. One of the explanations could be because of his view that, except a very special class of probabilities, probabilities in general are not numerically measurable. In this regard Schumpeter agreed with Keynes.

Additional justification for the discussion of probability theory by Keynes is that he (Keynes) thought it was mistaken Benthamite approach to probability and uncertainty that led to the mistaken theory of rate of interest by the classicists. Keynes (1937, 1969, P. 224) states this clearly.

The orthodox theory assumes that we have a knowledge of the future of kind quite different form that which we actually possess. This false realization follows the lines of Benthamite calculus. The hypothesis of a calculable future leads to a wrong inter-partition of the principals of behavior which the need for action compels us to adopt and to an underestimation of the concealed factors of utter doubt, precariousness, and fear. The result has been a mistaken theory of rate of rate of interest.

The above discussion substantiates the point that Keynes's theory of uncertainty and probability appertains to the economics of Keynes. Another relatively unexplored area of the economics of Keynes had been the strong bond that exists between Keynes' theory of probability and his views on enterprise. The statement below by Keynes (1936, p. 161) is quoted often but no connection has been established, to the best of my knowledge, between his theory of uncertainty and probability.

Most probably, of our decisions to do something positive, the full consequences of which will be drawn out over many days to come, can only be taken as a result of animal spirits-of a spontaneous urge to action rather than inaction, and not as the outcome of a weighted average of quantitative benefits multiplied by quantitative probabilities.

The following statement of Keynes (1936, p. 162) is akin to Schumpeter's view on enterprise.

Thus if animal spirits are dimmed and the spontaneous optimism falters, leaving us to defend on noting but a mathematical expectation, enterprise will fade and die; - though fears of loss may have a basis no more reasonable than hopes of profit had before.

It may be worth noting here that as far as this aspect of Keynes' view is concerned, it has not changed since he wrote *A Treatise On Money*. Identical views are echoed by Keynes (1930, 1971, Vol. 2, p. 132, 133) in the above book.

If enterprise is afoot, wealth accumulates whatever may be happening to thrift, and if enterprise is asleep, wealth decays whatever thrift may be doing. Thus thrift may be the handmaid and nurse of enterprise. But equally she may not. And, perhaps even usually, she is not. For enterprise is connected with thrift not directly but one remove; and link which should join them is frequently missing. For the engine which drives enterprise is not thrift, but profit.

It is interesting to point out that the two giants of economics—Frank H. Knight and Keynes—who would not agree on anything else except the definition and immeasurability of uncertainty. Knight (1921, p. 233) succinctly put it.

The practical difference between two categories, risk and uncertainty, is that in the former the distribution of the outcome in a group of instances is known (either through calculation a prior or from statistics of past experience), while in the case of uncertainty this is not true, the reason being in general that it is impossible to form a group of instances, because the situation dealt with is in a high degree unique.

As it is well known, according to Knight, profit is a reward for bearing uncertainty. The reasons for discussing Keynes's theory of probability at length are: (1) to show that economics of Keynes is not totally divorced from his theory of probability. In fact, the evidence presented above shows a vital link between the two, and (2) when it comes to the role of entrepreneur or Keynes' animal spirits, there is more similarity between them than apparently perceived or realized.

Chapter II of Schumpeter's *Theory of Economic Development* contains one of the best, if not the best, expositions of the dynamics of capitalism. It has the very pith of the spirit of Schumpeter's entrepreneur and his innovations. To clearly distinguish the role of the entrepreneur in the circular flow and development, Schumpeter (1934, pp. 79-80) uses the following analogy.

While he swims with the stream in the circular flow which is familiar to him, he swims against the stream if wishes to change its channel. What was familiar datum becomes an unknown.

Where the boundaries of routine stop, many people can go no further, and the rest can only do so in a highly variable manner. The assumption that conduct is prompt and rational is in all cases a fiction.

As can be seen in the above passage, Schumpeter is stating that what was routine and a familiar datum turns into an unknown. This implies that in innovating there is always uncertainty to be faced by the entrepreneur. The unknown or uncertainty inhibits ordinary people but the trail-blazing entrepreneur stridently strives on. The last sentence in the above passage is crucially important because here Schumpeter is challenging the traditional static neoclassical theory of the firm according to which the producer behaves rationally using the calculus of the marginal analysis to maximize profit. Schumpeter unhesitatingly and strongly states that such an assumption of rationality is a fiction in all cases. In such situations decisions undertaken are based on innate daring according to Schumpeter and animal spirits according to Keynes. No amount of rational investigation throws any light on the future uncertain events. Schumpeter (1934, p. 85) is very effective in expressing this thought.

Here the success of everything depends upon intuition, the capacity of seeing things in a way which afterwards proves to be true, even though it cannot be established at the moment, and of grasping the essential fact discarding the unessential, even though one can give no account of the principles by which this is done.

Like Keynes, Schumpeter also categorically rejects the notion of rationally calculating the probabilities. Both Keynes and Schumpeter would not subscribe to the present theories of uncertainty calculation.

Schumpeter's discussion of uncertainty is akin to Keynes's which is previously discussed. An entrepreneur could have subjective calculations but objective calculation of probabilities is not possible. According to Schumpeter, to an innovator many things remain uncertain. In Schumpeter's view acting routinely is like walking along a road whereas implementing an innovation is like making a road. Making a road, of course, involves facing obstacles or uncertainty.

In Schumpeter, there is a clear distinction drawn between risk and uncertainty. Schumpeter (1934, p. 195-196) clearly states that difference in relation to financial transactions.

For this purpose we only need to consider an addition for risk, which is known empirically, as included once for all in the "par price of the loan." This means that if it is known from experience that one percent of loans is irrecoverable then we shall say that the banker receives the same sum that he lent if he actually receives an additional 1.01 percent approximately from all debts which are not bad.

As the earlier discussion indicates that Schumpeter thought uncertainty was unknown in the sense that objective probabilities cannot be calculated. But risk he thought to empirically known, i.e., objective probabilities could be calculated. Separation of risk and uncertainty from the above point of view has played a significant role in the development of the science of economics, particularly in the development of the theory of profit. Professor Brahmananda (1983, October - December, Vol. 31) concurs with the view that Schumpeter was the earliest to distinguish between risk and uncertainty.

Further, Schumpeter was the earliest to distinguish between risk and uncertainty (between insurable risk and non-insurable uncertainty.)

Frank Knight is generally credited as the first one to distinguish between risk and uncertainty in his book. *Risk, Uncertainty and Profit*, 1921. The German edition of Schumpeter's *Theory of Economic Development* was published in 1912. This establishes the fact that Schumpeter was ahead of Knight in distinguishing risk and uncertainty. It must be pointed out here that we are not racing to establish Schumpeter's claim in this regard. Both Schumpeter and Knight are great economists and their claim to fame would not change an iota because of this. Besides there are many examples in the field of knowledge which show that two persons could independently hit on the same idea. General atmosphere in the process of the development of a science through the accretion of contributions by scholars gets charged and then the lightening strikes simultaneously or with a little difference of time at two places.

Keynes (1936, p. 150) agrees with Schumpeter's view that entrepreneurial decisions are not based on rational and cold calculations.

If human nature felt no temptation to take a chance, no satisfaction (profit apart) in constructing a factory, a railway, a mine or a farm, there might not be much investment merely as a result of cold calculation.

Unmistakable similarities exists between Keynes and Schumpeter when it comes to their comprehension and vision of the entrepreneurial functions. The same goes for their views concerning the nature and function of uncertainty. Entrepreneurial function and uncertainty are inseparably conjugated in the capitalistic reality according to both. The discussion of this topic can be capped by the following excerpts from (1) Schumpeter (1934 pp. 89-90) and Keynes (1936, p. 149 respectively.

(1) Add to this precariousness of the economic position both of individual entrepreneurs and of entrepreneur as a group..., and why scientific critique often makes short work of it.

(2) The outstanding fact is the extreme precariousness of the basis of knowledge on which our estimates of prospective yield have to be made. Our knowledge of the factors which will govern the yield of an investment some years hence is usually slight and often negligible.

The above presentation clinches the point concerning the concurrence of the views of Schumpeter and Keynes concerning entrepreneurial function and, risk and the uncertainty.

It would be interesting to find out how much mutually Schumpeter and Keynes influence each other. It would be totally incorrect to portray them as adversaries. Evidence presented above more than adequately proves that there are more similarities in their theories than some economists generally thought. Study of Keynes's *A Treatise on Money* readily reveals its authors familiarity with Schumpeter's ideas on innovator from the *Theory of Economic Development*. From a Keynes note on a reference to Schumpeter the only thing that is clear is Keynes studied the summary of Schumpeter done by Wesley Mitchell in his *Business Cycles*. There is no reference made to Schumpeter in *The General Theory*. Peter Drucker in his *Frontiers of Management* supplied evidence that strongly implies that Keynes was sufficiently familiar with Schumpeter's works and referred to them in his lectures. Drucker (1986, p. 105) clearly expresses this.

Keynes, in turn, considered Schumpeter one of the few contemporary economists worthy of his respect. In his lectures he again and again referred to the works Schumpeter had published during World War I, and especially to Schumpeter's essay on Rechenpfennige (that is, money of account) as the initial stimulus for his own thoughts on money. Keynes's most successful policy initiative, the proposal that Britain and the United States finance World War II by taxes rather than by borrowing, came directly out of Schumpeter's 1918 warning of the disastrous consequences of the debt financing of World War I.

Schumpeter's response to Keynes' *General Theory of Employment, Interest and Money* was characteristically of a scholar par excellence.

Despite his disagreement with Keynes on the certain aspects of theory and policy, Schumpeter encouraged his students at Harvard to study and to digest the *General Theory of Employment, Interest and Money*. Drucker's (1986, p. 105) statement below adduces to Schumpeter's greatness as a scholar.

> And although Schumpeter considered all Keynes' answers wrong, or at least misleading, he was a sympathetic critic. Indeed, it was Schumpeter who established Keynes in America. When Keynes's masterpiece, *General Theory of Employment, Interest and Money*, came out in 1936, Schumpeter, by then the senior member of the Harvard economic faculty, told his students to read the book and told them also that Keynes's work had totally superseded his own earlier writings on money.

The writings on money in the above statement refers, as can be reasoned, to theories of interest of Keynes and Schumpeter. As the previously presented evidence also indicates that Keynes was familiar with Schumpeter's work. Both think that interest rate is basically determined by the monetary forces and not by time preference and productivity.

Both Keynes and Schumpeter, unlike the classical and neoclassical economists, think that parsimony or thrift or saving is not as crucially important historically in capital formation. Harrod (1951 p. 405) appropriately expresses the classical and neoclassical view.

> Hither to the economists, as such, has tended to encourage economy and thrift in all circumstances.

Keynes from the days of *A Treatise on Money* did not subscribe to this view of the classicists and neoclassicists. According to Keynes (1930, 1971, p. 132), abstinence as such has not been the fountain of wealth.

> It has been usual to think of the accumulated wealth as having been painfully built up out of voluntary abstinence of individuals from the immediate enjoyment of consumption, which we call thrift. But it should be obvious that mere abstinence is not enough by itself to build cities or drain fens.

Schumpeter's view given below echoes the view that is identical in spirit with Keynes. He (Schumpeter) clearly states this (1934, p. 6).

> Different methods of employment, not saving and increase in the available quantity of labor, have changed the face of economic world in the last fifty years.

In Schumpeter's view creation of capital for economic development from saving out of the current or past saving is based on faulty economic analysis. Because in his circular flow system by definition there is no income available to save in a stationary state. Schumpeter (1934, p. 71) effectively expresses this point.

The accepted theory sees a problem in existence of the productive means, which are needed for new, or indeed any, productive processes, this accumulation therefore becomes a distinct function or service. We do not recognize this problem at all; it appears to us to be created by faulty analysis.

The agreement on this important aspect of economic theory and history between the two giants of twentieth century economics is certainly remarkable. Theories of economic development propounded by Arthur Lewis, Ragnar Nurkse and Walt Rostow put a heavy emphasis on capital formation in the process of development. But Simon Kuznets has taken a strong exception to the hypothesis that there was a sudden change in the rate of savings large enough for the take-off to use Rostow's catchy term. According to Kuznets the rate of savings required by Lewis and Rostow would have been impossible for the countries in the past. Kuznets (1974, p. 130) expresses his view.

Whatever the reason, the essential point is that even the richest countries of the world today, with a wealth and capacity far beyond the imagination of our forebears even in the late eighteenth and nineteenth century, raise the capital formation proportions to only moderate levels - indeed to levels that, on the net saving side, many earlier societies might have found not impossible and perhaps not even too difficult, to attain.

It must be understood that Kuznets is not agreeing with Keynes and Schumpeter. The relevant germane point for the discussion here is that on the basis of the historical experience high rate of saving has not been overwhelmingly crucial in economic development. The question that needs to be answered is if it is not the saving and consequent capital formation that generates economic growth according to Keynes and Schumpeter then what is it? The answer is that it is the enterprise or the animal spirits. Views of Keynes and Schumpeter concerning entrepreneurial function has been discussed adequately in the preceding discussion. Any addition to that would only be redundant.

4 Integration of money – Keynes and Schumpeter

The next important similarity between Keynes and Schumpeter is the integration of money into their system. Schumpeter must be considered a pioneer in this regard. Schumpeter was emancipated very early on from what Keynes calls in Chapter 21 of his *General Theory* as this "double life" of the separation of the theory of money and the theory of value and distribution. Keynes calls it a false dichotomy. Schumpeter's performance in this regard is nothing short of a flash of genius garnished in the historical congruity. Schumpeter was able to encapsulate the process of theory creation in his *History of Economic Analysis* on the basis of his own experience of creation of *The Theory of Economic Development*. It is Schumpeter's vision of the process of capitalistic dynamics.

In economics, monetary theory has always been controversial because it has to have its anchor in reality. Other economic theory tends to be deductio-hypothetical and, consequently, its ratiocination becomes highly moot and abstract. Monetary theory cannot afford such a luxury. Robert Clower (1969, p. 7) appropriately records this predicament of monetary theory.

In truth, contemporary monetary theory is among the least-settled branches of economic analysis and no serious student of modern economics can afford to be ignorant of this fact - or of the reasons for it.

The reason for this phenomenon is that the development of monetary thought is very history-bound. Keynes's *General Theory* was a response to the challenge of the Great Depression. Ricardo's contributions to monetary theory were related to the inflation existing during the Napoleonic wars. Inevitable policy prescriptions that follow the monetary theory also gives it an ideological charge. For example, the current controversy regarding monetary theory comes as an integral part of the total package. Money, especially its credit form, is to Schumpeter an inseparable ingredient of the capitalistic dynamics. In this regard, Schumpeter's view is akin to David Hume.

Accordingly we find that in every kingdom, into which money begins to flow in greater abundance than formerly, everything takes on a new face; labor and industry gain life; the merchant becomes more enterprising, and even the farmer follows his plough with greater alacrity and attention.

Further reading of Hume clearly indicates that he was shrewd enough to realize that the increase in money supply will not increase the real goods and services indefinitely. According to him the process will continue till the increased money supply will be in proportion to the real in GNP. This is expressing David Hume in modern terminology.

Schumpeter would wholeheartedly concur with Hume in regard to the effect of the increased money supply. But it must be stated that this is but a part of the story for Schumpeter. To him behind all these happenings, there is a doer - the entrepreneur. It is the entrepreneur's will that activates the process of innovations. But procurement of credit is absolutely necessary when the innovator wants to carry out new combination. Established firms in the stationary state cannot do this from the returns from the previous production. Borrowing is not a necessary element of production in the circular flow. But in carrying out new combinations and the financing of these new combinations is fundamentally necessary according to Schumpeter (1934, p. 70.)

The capitalistic credit system has grown out of and thrived on the financing of new combinations in all countries, even though in a different way in each (the origin of German joint stock banking is especially characteristic). Finally there can be no stumbling block in our speaking of receiving credit in "money or money substitutes."

Highly elastic credit supply that is necessary to put in motion the wheels of capitalism is created by the banker in the Schumpeterian system. To Schumpeter, banker is not simply a middleman between savers and investors. He is the capitalist, who serves as a differentia specifica and who aids in forcing the economic system into new channels. Schumpeter (1934., p. 7) describes the role of a banker.

The banker, therefore, is not so much primarily a middleman in the commodity "purchasing power" as a producer of this commodity. However, since all reserve funds and savings today usually flow to him, and the total demand for free purchasing power, whether existing or to be created, concentrates on him, he has either replaced private capitalist or become their agent; he has himself become the capitalist par excellence.

As far as Schumpeter's monetary theory foundations are concerned he does not fully agree with either the Currency School or the Banking School, though his sympathies would definitely lie on the side of the Banking School. His major objection to both the theories is their emphasis on banks mainly financing current, routine and short-term loans. Both the theories according to Schumpeter are below the mark because they fail to assign the proportional importance to credit creation by the banks for innovations. In Schumpeter's vision the banks create credit to finance innovations. The loans to entrepreneurs need not be repaid in the sense that they are reviewed in such a way as to augment the money supply. Once the economic system is in full motion, due to innovations, the major part of the bank credit outstanding is absorbed in current business and looses its contact with innovation. The secondary impulses that follow the original processes are consumers borrowing on the one hand, and saving on the other. This secondary aspect is emphasized and canonized by the banking theory, in which the original process of innovation—the essence of capitalism is lost sight off—and also forgotten. The original drama that starts the whole thing fades away in oblivion and never to be surfaced. To Schumpeter this is inexcusable because it gets obliterated and the direction of causation in economic theory is misdirected. The thing (innovation and credit creaction) causes everything (capitalistic development) is never thought to be the cause of it. The total emphasis on routine has imparted the static orientation to the economic theory, and when the dynamics was introduced, it was by applying difference or differential equation (dating of quantities) to the routine. The real cause is thrown further in oblivion.

In spite of his criticism of both the Banking and Currency Schools, Schumpeter finds certain elements of The Banking School palatable and he (1964, p. 90) adequately expresses this.

It is important for the functioning of the system that the banker should know, and be able to judge, what his credit is used for and that he should be an independent agent. To have stressed it at least by implication, is one of the chief merits of the commercial theory of banking (The Banking School), just as it is one of the chief demerits of the investment theory (The Currency School)—which is a typical outsider's idea and could never, like its rival, have grown out of practical banking experience—to have overlooked it and to have made banking a mechanical function which might just as well be filled by some government department.

If entrepreneur, innovation, credit creation and the personal involvement in credit-granting by the banker are integrated into the process of development, Schumpeter's Theory can be meshed with the Banking School and its real bills doctrine. According to the Banking School, a mixed currency will expand and contract with the needs of business and a bank's assets will normally consist of "real-bills". The Banking School based the validity of real-bills doctrine on a Law of Reflex: if the banks should lend excessively for speculative purposes regardless of the real-bills, increase in prices will create a run on the banks for conversion into specie. This is a built-in safeguard against inflation. Application of the above to the Schumpeterian system would involve the following scenario. First, unlike the general drift of the English classical economics, personal involvement of the entrepreneur and banker is important to Schumpeter. The English classical economists, following Adam Smith, have chosen to emphasize the "invisible hand" or the impersonal forces of the market. Schumpeter (1964, p. 90) is quite clear on this point.

Even if he (the banker, added) confines himself to the most regular of commodity bills and looks with aversion on any paper that displays a suspicious round figure, the banker must not only know what the transaction is which he is asked to finance and how it is likely to turn out, but he must also know the customer, his business, even his private habits and get, by frequently "talking things over with him," a clear picture of his situation. But if bank finance innovation, all this becomes immeasurably more important. It has been denied that such knowledge is possible. The reply is that all banks who at all answer to type, have it and act upon it. The giant banking concerns of England have their organs or subsidiaries which enable them to carry on that old tradition: the necessity of looking after customers and constantly feeling their pulse is one of the reasons for the division of labor between the big banks and the discount houses in the London money market.

Once perfect capital or money market is assumed, in accordance with Adam Smith, the banker's involvement and entrepreneur's role in innovations become inadmissible. Schumpeter, as the remarks above indicate, is aware of the unpalatability of the active role of the banker and entrepreneur in the ambit of the static model of perfect competition. To drive his point home, he has given an illustration of the English capital and money market. This lengthy digression has become necessary to clarify the differences between Schumpeter and classical economists.

The Banking School theory now can be applied to Schumpeterian situation. Innovator conceives the idea of a new product, process, market, source of raw material and organization. The banker willingly finances the venture by creating credit (real bills) upon judging the soundness of the project. The banker has the intimate knowledge of the relevant factors involved in innovation. The banker is the capitalist who is willing, on the basis of his knowledge, to supply the required purchasing power to create disequilibrium by pulling resources out of the static circular flow. In fact, it is because of the banker's substantial knowledge surrounding the project, the product, the potential market, technology and aspects of entrepreneur's personal traits, he (the banker) is ready to create credit. It is the soundness of the venture that necessitates the creation of credit or real bills. Credit or money is created on the basis of the needs of trade. It can be now judged that Schumpeter's objection to the Baking School theory can be overcome and recast to fit the Schumpeter's situation. Schumpeter's objection, as can be recalled, was centered on two points as far as the Banking School theory is concerned. First, according to him, the Banking School theory dealt only with the routine financing. It is shown above that with the minimum of stretching the Banking School Theory can be subsumed into the Schumpeterian system.

Second, the next important point of concern is how far can the process of credit creation continue without precipitation into a serious inflation. According to Schumpeter, the banks in order not to endanger their solvency will voluntarily restrain credit in such a way that the resulting inflation will be mild and of short duration. Schumpeter (1934, p. 113) states this clearly.

And if solvency of the banking system in this sense not to be endangered, the banks can only give credit in such a way that the resulting inflation is really temporary and moreover remains moderate.

As far as the potentiality of inflation due to credit creation by the banks is concerned, the following additional points, which are likely to serve as the dampers on inflation, should be seriously considered.

On the basis of linking of the Schumpeterian theory of credit creation to the real-bills doctrine, it can be argued that credit created by the banker, on the basis of his intimate knowledge, only when it is potentially matched by the augmented output of goods and services. It can also be discerned on the basis of the discussion so far that the Law Reflux of the Banking School and Schumpeter's view of the banks voluntarily restraining credit to safeguard solvency of the banks are similar or least close. Schumpeter (1964, p. 13) states that because the amount of credit needed to initiate innovation is not large enough to be inflationary.

This we shall not do, since even a small amount of credit creation suffices to produce the phenomena we have been describing.

Besides, the investment that follows after the successful innovation is financed from savings that is done out of the earned profits. The original act of credit credit creation has played itself out and the secondary investment is done by the business out of the profits earned. Of the total credit created, relatively small magnitude seeps gradually into the economy according to Schumpeter. Moreover, not all banks expand credit simultaneously. According to him no precise limit can be set to credit creation beforehand, and in practice, might be determined by the legislation and temperament of the people.

Both Keynes and Schumpeter want to emphasize and integrate money in their theories. But the difference between their monetary theories is too wide. According to Schumpeter emergence of the banker and the credit economy, along with the entrepreneur and his innovation, represents the body and soul of capitalism. Schumpeter wants to explain the dynamic, evolutionary and pulsating transformation of the feudal society of Europe into capitalism, which could not have been materialized without the banker's credit creation. Keynes's main objective in the *General Theory* is to forge the theory of the monetary economy in which rate of interest, employment, prices, output and incomes were determined. Compartmentalization of economics into value and monetary theory was too glaring. Austin Robinson's (1985, p. 56) statement below depicts the situation.

The second thing I think came out of the thanking of the Circus was really the integration of value theory and monetary theory into what we now call macroeconomics, but did not have the name before then. I as an undergraduate listened to Pigou's lectures on value theory. Then I cycled across the town to listen to Henderson on monetary theory. There was complete schizophrenia at that time between the two sets of lectures. You could make any proposition you liked about monetary policies on the assumption that it had no effect whatsoever on actual output.

These are strong words but they are also a pointer to what Keynes was after. Keynes thought there was a lack of monetary theory of production. Most of the treatises on principles of economics mainly, if not entirely, dealt with a real exchange economy. The distinction was usually made between a barter economy and a monetary economy. In a monetary economy, money was treated as an instrument of great convenience with transitory and neutral effects. Keynes definitely wanted to go beyond. Keynes (1973, p. 408) states this in no uncertain terms.

> The theory which I desiderate would deal in contradiction to this, with an economy in which money plays a part of its own and affects motives and decisions and is, in short, one of the operative factors in the situation, so that the course of events cannot be predicted, either in long period or in the short, without a knowledge of the behavior of the money between the first state and the last. And it is this which we ought to mean when we speak of a monetary economy.

As can be discerned from the above statement, Schumpeter would have no quarrel with the spirit of the quotation, especially, when it concerns motives and decisions and operative factors. But the similarity cannot be stretched beyond this point. Schumpeter is analyzing and revealing the propelling impulses of a system that is continuously becoming (metamorphosing). Keynes has laid down the foundations of the theory of the output and employment. It is interesting to note that both Keynes and Schumpeter are not concerned with the traditional allocation of branch of the economic theory. As far as the allocation branch is concerned Keynes's position is ambivalent or least not clearly stressed. Schumpeter's position is clear. According to Schumpeter imperfect competition and monopolies will emerge but will not survive.

Initially there is a similarity between Keynes's and Schumpeter's bankers. Both are capitalists.

The state of the monetary theory after Keynes and Schumpeter, despite of the development of powerful mathematical tools, had not advanced. The very existence of money proves to be a hurdle in this case. The state of the art model—the Arrow-Debreu format of a Walrasian general equilibrium—cannot in-corporate money into itself. Arrow-

Debreu model, in which future contracts exist on contingency basis, makes money unnecessary and unwanted. Incorporation of money in it is not possible because of uncertainty factor. With uncertainty present, the Arrow-Debreu model would not be Pareto-efficient. Frank Hahn (1983, p. 1) succinctly puts this.

The most serious challenge that existence of money poses to the theorist is this: the best developed model of the economy cannot find room for it. The best developed model is, of course, the Arrow-Debreu version of a Walrasian general equilibrium. A world in which all conceivable contingent future contracts are possible neither needs nor wants intrinsically worthless money. A first and to a fastidious theorist difficult task is to find an alternative construction without thereby sacrificing the clarity and logical coherence that are such outstanding features of Arrow-Debreu.

What money is supposed to do is all assumed away in the highly developed Arrow-Debreu system. The conjugation of the value and monetary theory has not consummated yet. As pointed out earlier, this was the desire of Keynes. The crux of the problem is pointed out clearly by Arrow and Hahn (1971, p. 338).

Of course, our mode is in no shape to give satisfactory formal account of the role of money. In particular, it would be "hard to explain" the holding of money or why it mediates in most acts of exchange. For the moment, we sidestep these portentous issues by making assumptions of a simple pure-exchange economy, are not altogether off the mark in a more satisfactory and complicated world. The first thing to notice is that if some commodity called money indeed must mediate exchange, this in itself yet damage our conclusion of the previous section if we can take it that sales and purchases are simultaneous. In this case, there is no "first leg" and "second leg" of a transaction and we could continue to postulate that every transaction is of a kind that does not decrease the utility of the transactors. If this is the case, however, we certainly would be hard put to explain why any household should hold any money at all (here, of course we are abstracting from price uncertainty).

Despite the differences of the details as far as their views on monetary theory are concerned, Keynes and Schumpeter agree strongly on integrating money into general economic analysis. That is the common ground they both share. Like Keynes, Schumpeter also is acutely aware of the sharp difference that did exist in the treatment of the real and the monetary economy. Schumpeter (1954, pp. 277-78) also states that monetary factors do affect real factors. Schumpeter gives illustration of California gold discoveries by strongly implying that these discoveries did substantially move the real economy besides raising the price level. Like Adam Smith, he also believes that the development of an efficient banking system does contribute significantly to the augment a country's wealth. Study of monetary analysis according to Schumpeter introduces an element of reality in economic theory. Capitalist process and reality cannot be adequately understood by the study of the barter economy in Schumpeter's view. At this point it is appropriate to let Schumpeter (1954, p. 278) state his views.

We are thus led, step by step, to admit monetary elements into real analysis and to doubt that money can ever be neutral in any meaningful sense. In the second place, then, monetary analysis introduces the element of money on the ground floor of our analytical structure and abandons the idea that all essential features of economic life can be represented by a barter-economy mode. Money prices, money incomes, and savings and investment decisions bearing upon these money incomes, no longer appear as expressions—sometimes convenient, sometimes misleading, but always nonessential of quantities and commodities and services and of exchange ratios between them: they acquire a life and importance of their own, and it has to be recognized that essential features of the capitalist process may depend upon the "veil" and the face 'behind it' is incomplete without it. It should be stated once for all that as a matter of fact this is almost universally recognized by modern economists, at least in principle, and that, taken in this sense Monetary Analysis has established itself.

Schumpeter writing the above in 1954 was justified in saying that monetary analysis has established itself. In the light of the foregone discussion of the monetary theories of Schumpeter and Keynes, it would be appropriate at this time to examine the current monetary theory of rational expectations. Keynes introduced expectations in economic analysis in his General Theory. Hicks in his Value and Capital attempted to formalize, though not very satisfactorily, expectations in general equilibrium theory. Being consummate theorists both Keynes and Schumpeter would heartily welcome the current sophisticated theory of rational expectations with its accomplished craftsmanship. But both would not approve of the implications of the theory of rational expectations concerning the monetary theory. Because the theory of rational expectations re-establishes the classical monetary theory with full vigor and with the powerful mathematical and statistical tools.

According to the theory of rational expectations, individual decision makers are rational maximizing units and all markets are instantaneously cleared to establish equilibrium price vector at which excess demand is eliminated. This theory is first expressed by J. F. Muth in 1961 in its well-developed logical form in his study of the price behavior of security and commodity markets. Muth seeks an answer to the question as to why no rule, formula or model has ever been consistently successful in forecasting prices in financial markets which seem to resemble a "random walk" process on which noise is superimposed. His reply was, in effect, that all available information capable of maximizing the accuracy of price forecasts is almost instantaneously included into current decisions by speculators, whose predictions and hence expectations are "rational" in this precise sense. In the 1970's, the traditional Keynesian demand management macroeconomic economic policies turned out to be relatively less effective in solving the twin problem of unemployment and inflation in the United States. R.E. Lucas Jr., T. J. Sargent and N. Wallace simultaneously thought of applying Muth's theory of rational expectations to the macroeconomic problems. The gist of the theory is that economic agents form their expectations on the basis of exactly the identical information that is utilized by the policy formulators and, hence expectation of price changes in the same way that the market determines actual prices. This does not rule out the possibility of mistaken expectations because the foresight is not perfect and the economy might be subject to random and unexpected shocks. But the mean or mathematical expectation of subjective expectations of price variables will be the same as of objective expectations in terms of probability distributions. In short, expected error of rational forecast or prediction is always zero.

The question from Keynes's point of view to the rational expectationists would be what causes serious deviations from full employment and general equilibrium? It is caused by random error and not by the deficiency of aggregate demand according to the rational expectationists. Lapses from full employment are caused by the deficiency of aggregate demand according to Keynes. Rational expectationists' argument is akin to the Chicago School, a la Friedman, argument that the real economic activity is inherently stable. This is like stealing the whole thunder of Keynes's message, which is precisely what the rational expectationists want to do. In fact, the very reincarnation of the new classical economics (rational expectations hypothesis) is to annihilate economics of Keynes.

There also cannot be any endearment between Schumpeter and the rational expectationists. According to Schumpeter, business cycles are caused by the entrepreneur's innovational activity, credit creation by the banks and the herd-like behavior of the secondary entrepreneurs. None of these have any place in the business cycle theory of the rational expectationists. According to the rational expectationists, business cycles are caused by the limited information imparted by the price signals to the rational decision makers. This needs some elaboration. In view of the rational expectationists, there is a difference in relative speed at which suppliers imbibe information concerning the prices at which they sell and at which they buy. The unanticipated rise in prices is mistakenly thought to be a rise in the relative price of what they sell and consequently supply more. Increased output is materialized because everybody on average perceives the same increase in relative price. But subsequently mistake is realized by everybody and they retreat from supplying more consequently, the aggregate output is reduced to its original level. Schumpeter would view such as an explanation of business cycles as superficial and utterly devoid of capitalistic reality of innovations leading to shifts in production functions and a perpetual gale of creative destruction. He would consider such an explanation of business cycles as ad hock without any real substance in it. Schumpeter would say that this explanation of business is like a person who after studying the New Testament does not know who Jesus Christ is or at the most he is a minor character in it. This might sound like over dramatization but upon consideration of Schumpeter's view of business cycles it is justified. To Schumpeter, business cycles are (1) caused by the mixture of real and monetary factors, (2) intertwined with economic growth and (3) part and parcel of capitalism. Moreover, as noted above, in Schumpeter's view to regard economic processes, particularly the process of innovation, as rational and prompt is in all cases close to fiction.

5 The role of imperfect competition – Keynes and Schumpeter

An area of economic theory in which similarity between Keynes and Schumpeter does exists, though Keynes never agreed to this as the evidence presented below shows, is the theory of imperfect competition Schumpeter's views on the theory of imperfect competition are quite well known. Roy Harrod, an oxford economist, tried to draw Keynes' attention to some of the latent implications of the *General Theory* which could logically support arguments for the theory of imperfect competition went unheeded by Keynes. This line of thought is successfully pursued by Michael Kalecki who is strongly supported by Joan Robinson.

The nature of Schumpeter's theoretical framework is highly conducive to the theory of imperfect competition. Schumpeter uses the notion of circular flow and the world of perfect competition as a starting point. But it also carries a significance with it because activity and impulses that propel economic development cannot theoretically occur in the stationary world of perfect competition. To innovate is to break out of the channel of the circular flow according to Schumpeter (1934, p. 152).

Since the entrepreneur has no competitors when the new products first appear, the determination of their price proceeds wholly, or within certain limits, according to the principles of monopoly price. Thus there is monopoly element in profit in a capitalistic economy.

Schumpeter very carefully distinguishes profit as an income that accrues to the entrepreneur in the capitalist system. Profit exists in the capitalist system as a reward for innovation and continues to exist as long as the entrepreneur continues to innovate. Like wages, profit is not a permanent branch of income. Innovation creates surplus which did not exist in a stationary economy. This surplus is an entrepreneurial profit. Profit lasts as long as entrepreneur's monopoly lasts, and this monopoly position of the entrepreneur does not last very long. Profit slips away from the entrepreneur's grasp as soon as the entrepreneurial function is performed according to Schumpeter. In summary, temporary monopoly of the entrepreneur exits because of innovation and temporary profit exists because of monopoly.

When a new method of production is developed, the aim of such a method is to lower the unit cost of production through the larger scale of production. Schumpeter is fully aware of the entailing consequences of the role of imperfect competition in his system, especially the role of imperfect competition in the various phases of business cycles. Following are the consequences he recognizes. First, he surmises that the elements of indeterminates of the equilibrium will be introduced due to the oligopoly situations. As a consequence of the above, he thinks that the system will be slowed down in speed in its move towards the equilibrium. Secondly, unlike the world of perfection competition, there will be more room for the plays of entrepreneurial moves and counter-moves which will pave the way towards equilibrium. Third, Schumpeter (1964, p. 137) aware of the fact, though he does not state it elaborately, that market imperfections might create excess capacity resulting into unemployment. But it must be emphasized here that Schumpeter is totally unwilling, as can be understood later on the basis of the logic of his theory, to build a theory of business cycles around it. Schumpeter (1964, p. 137) is very forthright on this issue.

Since it has with many economists has become a fashion to make the presence of unemployed resources—labor, in particular,—a datum of the problem of cycles, to base their theories on it and to object to other theories on the ground that they neglect, we will state once more where we stand concerning this matter. Imperfections of both competition and equilibrium, as well as external disturbances, may account for the presence of unemployed resources independently of the cyclical process of evolution.

Schumpeter thinks that his own system produces market imperfections and disequilibria which produces unemployment that could outlast the unemployment generated by other factors. Part of unemployment created by market imperfections does represent a disequilibrium from full employment according to Schumpeter. But the disequilibrium Schumpeter is interested in is the one created by innovations. Schumpeter (1942) re-enforces his views with fineness and maturity in his *Capitalism, Socialism and Democracy*. Schumpeter (1942, p. 84) is happy to see that economist are abandoning their tunnel-vision of perfect competition and are integrating the vital elements such as quality competition and sales efforts into the scared precincts of the economic theory. He also takes cognizance of the fact that the foundations of the allocation branch based on the doctrine of perfect competition are shaken by the theoretical development of the theory of imperfect and monopolistic competition. Schumpeter thinks that a more serious blow to the doctrine of perfect competition will be delivered by the developments in dynamic analysis. This hope of Schumpeter has not come true. As a theoretical norm, perfect competition still reigns supreme.

As far as Keynes is concerned, certain elements of his analysis in general theory are hospitable to the idea of imperfect competition but as the evidence will show that he also does not think, like Schumpeter in this narrow sense, that depression was caused by market imperfections, particularly by the phenomenon of increasing returns. Harrod unsuccessfully tried to convince Keynes to introduce this element in his *General Theory*.

Piero Sraffa in his famous 1926 paper, "The Laws of Returns Under Competitive Condition" challenged the traditional analysis of supply based on the law of diminishing returns. Sraffa argues that application of the law of diminishing returns is justified in agriculture as it is done by the classical economists in the analysis of supply. But in manufacturing or non-agricultural situation in which scope for expanding division of labor exists, the analysis of supply should be based on increasing returns. The reason such an application had been avoided up to that time was that it was incompatible with the equilibrium under perfect competition. Sraffa's contribution stimulated major research in this area which culminated in the development of the theory of imperfect and monopolistic competition. Harrod's work on imperfect competition was also inspired by the same source.

The relevance of the preceding development in Harrod's view is more to macroeconomics than to microeconomics. Harrod has known of Keynes's interest in the problems of unemployment. Harrod has known from his conversations with the producers that increase in demand for their products would further lower their average costs. This matches Keynes's theory of lack of effective demand. Increase in aggregate demand will let the firms produce more at lower average costs which will also increase employment. Consequently, employment increases and output increases without inflation. Harrod's idea is very much unlike the classical, Keynesian, Keynes's and neoclassical. At this stage in our argument, it is worth citing Harrod (1967, p. 74-75).

For me the matter was more of a sideline. It was particularly concerned with the subject of increasing returns. During the twenties many of us were deeply interested in Keynes's advocacy of measurement to promote fuller employment. According to the traditional theory, success of this would entail higher marginal costs and lower real wages. And yet there was a great paradox. If an academic economist left his ivory tower and mingled a little with industrialists in the field he could not help being impressed with the fact that the great majority of these industrialists affirmed that they could produce more at lower cost, both in the long and in the short period, if only they had a bigger demand to satisfy. There seemed to be a stark contradiction between the views of the industrialists and the theory of perfect competition. And of course, if the industrialists were right, this would be helpful for Keynesian policy.

The Harrod hypothesis, if true, has the following significant implications. First, in terms of Okun's terminology, the difference between actual and potential GNP should be much larger. Second, the full employment ceiling in the Hicksian cycle should be much higher. Third, the aggregate supply curve will be slightly negatively sloping over a large part of output as depicted in Figure 5.1 below.

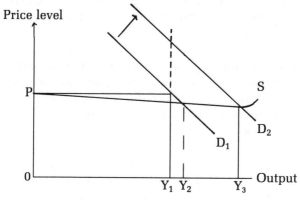

Figure 5.1

The negative slope of the Harrodian aggregate supply will depend on the number of the firms in the economy having decreasing marginal costs as the output increases. If substantial majority of firms have decreasing marginal costs and the decrease itself is substantial, the Harrodian aggregate supply will be more inelastic.

Despite Harrod's persuasion, Keynes remained committed to the idea of diminishing returns—at least in the short run. His (Harrod's) disappointment concerning this point was completely eclipsed by the excitement created by the unorthodox ideas in Keynes's *General Theory*. Harrod (1967, p. 75) expresses this in the following way.

> All these considerations were somewhat lost sight of when Keynes's *General Theory* appeared. In that book he seemed to accept—lock, stock barrel—the assumption of diminishing returns, at least in short period. I recall being disappointed about this, but such a minor disappointment was overlaid by the great intellectual excitement and enthusiasm by that volume.

Harrod thinks, at best, the issue of increasing returns should be regarded as unsettled as far as manufacturing activity is concerned. He thinks that there does not seem to have an established correlation in recent years in England between the variations of the prices of manufactured goods and intensity of manufacturing activity. This is an empirically testable proposition.

Harrod was not successful in convincing Keynes in integrating imperfect competition in his system. Keynes (Harcourt, 1985, p. 69) in a reply to Harrod concerning this point expresses his views as follows.

> I have not been able to make out here what you are driving at. The reference to imperfect competition is very perplexing. I cannot see how on earth it comes in. Mrs. Robinson, I may mention, read my proofs without discovering any connection..... I have always regarded decreasing physical returns as one of the very few incontrovertible propositions of our miserable subject! I should have thought that employment never did fall materially without a rise in real hourly wage. Is this not one of the best established of statistical conclusions?

Keynes' reservations and final denial of Harrod's argument concerning imperfect competition could be due to (1) Keynes' help to his student, Richard Kahn, in his King's Fellowship dissertations to construct a positively sloping supply curve for cotton yarn, and (2) the doctrine of excess capacity, an outcome of Chamberlin's famous tangency solution under monopolistic competition. Admission of imperfect competition would have meant that less than full employment output could be explained by market imperfections which is a generally accepted proposition in economics. Keynes must have realized, as others did, incorporating imperfect competition would deny or at least dilute the role of effective demand in his analysis.

It must be pointed out that Keynes missed the full import of Harrod's argument. The doctrine of excess capacity has gotten firmly implanted in economic theory despite the strident efforts against its happening by Harrod and Kaldor. Harrod unsuccessfully tried to convince Keynes at the time The General Theory was being incubated. Kaldor (1935) has severely criticized Chamberlin's tangency solution and have attempted to demonstrate that with the threat of potential entrants and increasing returns entrepreneurs will end up with the competitive price and output.

As usual, a perceptible remark on Schumpeter made by Samuelson (1986, p. 301) is correct. Samuelson in his remark touches the very persona of Schumpeter. He (Samuelson) states that the Wagnerian hero, which is what Schumpeter would have liked to be, does not strive to be a Jack-of-all-trades and Schumpeter would have gladly forsaken, what Samuelson calls Popeship, for a Keynesian revolution. This remark is correct because as pointed out before that according to Peter Drucker some of Schumpeter's students were told by Schumpeter that he (Schumpeter) was planning to create a theoretical work similar to General Theory and Keynes's contribution superseded what Schumpeter intended. If this remark concerning Schumpeter's conception of an embryo, which was not fully incubated is true, then Schumpeter, like a Wagnerian hero, planned the heroic act. But like some other things in life, it is all in timing. Alas Schumpeter was late. The option of joining the Keynesian revolution was still open to Schumpeter which he chose not to because, maybe, he did not want to be an imitator or a Wagnerian hero in Keynesian limelight.

When Samuelson's analysis and diagnosis is juxtaposed to Peter Drucker's (1986, pp. 104-115) diametrically opposite prognosis emerges. According to Drucker, in the long run Schumpeterian vision and concern will be of vital importance for economic theory and policy. Persistence of innovations and entailing technological change propelled by adequate profits to maintain full employment with healthy growth have been at the vital center of Schumpeter's thinking. Drucker also points out that in Schumpeter's economics, unlike the classical and Keynesian economics, innovation and technological change are an integral part. In Drucker's view Schumpeter is totally opposed to the short-term fine-tuning and short-term optimization of the economy through intervention. Drucker juxtaposes Keynes and Schumpeter in the following way.

In some ways Keynes and Schumpeter replayed the best-known confrontation of philosophers in the Western tradition—the Platonic dialogue between Parmendies, the brilliant, clever, irresistible sophist, and the slow-moving and ugly, but wise Socrates. No one in the interwar years was more brilliant, more clever than Keynes. Schumpeter, by contrast, appeared pedestrian—but he had wisdom. Cleverness carries the day. But wisdom endureth.

Only time will tell if Drucker's prophesy will be fulfilled totally or partially, but the uniqueness of Schumpeterian system in terms of entrepreneurial function, innovation, the dynamic competition and the gale of creative destruction will endure. Certain elements in Schumpeter such as different and better utilization of resources as dynamic impulses of growth have place in the literature and reality of growth and development. One of the areas of Schumpeter's contribution overlooked by economists is his linking of an innovator and areas of firm's operation. Schumpeter painstakingly grooms his analysis of innovation which could occur in marketing, production, finance, management and human relations. Schumpeter's superstructure is firmly founded on the microfoundations of the firm. Marshall grappled with this aspect of economics in his *Trade and Industry* but he (Marshall) has not used it as an instrument of dynamic analysis to investigate capitalism.

To be fair to Schumpeter, he must be studied in depth and breadth. Schumpeter is determined to reveal the very life-force of capitalism. What Keynes thinks to be shortcoming of capitalism, to Schumpeter it is but a lapse. There is a mover in the system, the entrepreneurs, his will acts as a dynamo, his will is manifested through the instrumentality of innovations and reward for fulfillment of the will is profit. When looked at it this way, it is not much different from the magnificent dynamics of Adam Smith. The entrepreneur's selfish pursuit of profit ends up creating social good, e.g., new goods, new methods of production, etc. which is none of his intention. Despite Schumpeter, it is worth quoting from Plato's *Timaeus* (1961, p. 1183). It is said despite Schumpeter because in his *History of Economic Analysis*, (pp. 53-55), Schumpeter does not think much of Plato as an economist. The quotation below from Plato fits Schumpeter's conception and vision of capitalist process.

Unless a person comes to an understanding about the nature and conditions of rest and motion, he will meet with many difficulties in the discussion which follows. Something has been said of this matter already, and something more remains to be said—which is that motion never exists in what is uniform. For to conceive that anything can be moved without a mover is hard or indeed impossible, and equally impossible to conceive that there can be a mover unless there is something which can be moved—motion cannot exist where either of these is wanting, and for these to be uniform is impossible; wherefore we must assign rest to uniformity and motion to the want of uniformity.

To complete the analogy, Schumpeter's circular flow is what is uniform in which motion in the sense of innovational changes does not exists. Motion or moving out of equilibrium of the circular flow occurs because there is a mover, that is the entrepreneur. The object to be moved is the economic system. But it is not like a mover moving an object from one place to the other. The move in Schumpeterian sense involves an organic, qualitative and irreversible motion. The truth of the matter is to an awakened and a trained human mind, there is an inexhaustible mine of scientific ideas out of which eventually technology evolves and as long as entrepreneurs and his quest for profit remains strong, there will be the evolving and expanding universe of capitalism in Schumpeterian sense. This is but a part of Schumpeter.

The other part comes from realizing profit potential from doing things differently and or efficiently.

Schumpeter has investigated into the deepest layers of the creative process of theorizing in economics. Before analytical outcome can manifest itself in a fuller form, according to Schumpeter, there is a preanalytic cognitive act precedes it. This preanalytic cognitive act supplies the building-blocks or raw materials for the theory. In economics the sources of raw materials are history, sociology, political science and statistics. Schumpeter (1954, p. 41) succinctly expresses this.

In other words, analytic effort is of necessity preceded by a preanalytic cognitive act that supplies the raw material for analytic effort. In this book, this preanalytic cognitive act is called Vision.

Vision is a key word in Schumpeter's process of theorizing and in his case historical experience is crucial. But here also there is a Schumpeterian twist. By historical experience Schumpeter implies broad concrete epoch-making events that impinge on economic life in a substantial way. Accretion to knowledge by infinitesimal steps from contemporaneous events may not be of much significance to a theorist. Events that are capable of generating a sustained wave-like motion in economic activity of an extended duration are crucial in Schumpeter's view. Schumpeter supplies an appropriate illustration when he (Schumpeter, 1935, p. 7) says that add as many mail-coaches as you please, you will never get a railroad by so doing. Historical facts such as the railroad from a part of Schumpeterian vision.

According to Schumpeter incessant change through innovations propelled by the entrepreneur in search of transient monopoly profit is capitalism's way. Schumpeter has adhered to this vision till the very end. Occurrence of the Great Depression was nothing extraordinary, as it was to Keynes and most of the Keynesians, and out of tune with capitalism in the historical sense. Schumpeter (1942, p. 64) puts it effectively.

> For the depression ran its course from last quarter of 1929 to the third quarter of 1932 does not prove that a secular break has occurred in the propelling mechanism of capitalist production because depressions of such severity have repeatedly occurred—roughly one in fifty years—and because of the effects of one of them—the one from 1873 to 1877—are taken account of in the annual average of 2 percent.

To Schumpeter growth and cycles are conjugated together in an inseparable way. Policies to eliminate or moderate fluctuations will inhibit innovations which serve as well-springs of economic growth. One cannot have growth without fluctuations. The above discussion taken together constitutes Schumpeter's answer to Keynes. The occurrence and severity of the Great Depression was not an historical break or unique. Taming of capitalism through governmental intervention is bound to make it languid. Referring back to the quotation from Plato, Schumpeter, like Plato, believes that uniformity, the circular flow in Schumpeterian sense, does not create motion. And the economic reality is not uniform. Innovations generate motion in economic activity. The mover is the entrepreneur. This is a part of Schumpeter's vision of capitalism.

Keynes had seen serious problems with capitalism in his *Economic Consequences of the Peace* and *The End of Laissez-faire* before writing *General Theory*. All three works by Keynes represent his criticism of the performance of the then existing order of capitalism. They do not provide the theoretical answer for the inadequate performance of capitalism which *General Theory* does. The answer is the lack of effective demand. An economic system based on profit motive cannot self-equilibrate if aggregate demand falls short of aggregate supply. Keynes's and Schumpeter's views can be juxtaposed with the analogy of the half-full glass. Schumpeter is saying the glass is half full and far from being empty. The historical performance of capitalism is impressive and capitalism has managed to create unparalleled increase in the material standard of living and will continue to do so if certain forces, of its own doing, do not inhibit it. Schumpeter (1942, p. 67) states this remarkably well.

> The capitalist achievement does not typically consists in providing more silk stocking for the queens but in bringing them within the reach of factory girls in return for steadily decreasing amounts of efforts.

Schumpeter's statement congeals the very essence of the end product of the process of capitalism.

Keynes, as opposed to Schumpeter, says that the glass is half empty and is being emptied fast. Keynes (1936, p. 372) put it effectively.

> The outstanding faults of the economic society in which we live are its failure to provide for full employment and its arbitrary and inequitable distribution of wealth and incomes.

6 Application of Stigler's criteria – Keynes and Schumpeter

According to Stigler (1965, p. 34) great economists are the ones who influence the profession as a whole, and the doctrines they promulgate enrich the existing knowledge in better understanding the reality... Scientific originality in its important role should be measured against the knowledge of a man's contemporaries. If he opens their eyes to new ideas or to new perspective on old ideas, he is an original economist in the scientifically important sense.

On the basis of Stigler's criteria, Schumpeter certainly can be called a great economist with originality. The pith of Schumpeter's ideas concerning innovations, the role of an entrepreneur, economic progress being not linear but the one which comes in spurts mainly generated in booms, and fusion of growth and cycles have permeated into corpus of the economic theory. Schumpeter also will be remembered as a creator of phases such as creative destruction profitless prosperities, imitating entrepreneurs, and shifting of production function.

R.M. Goodwin (1965, p. 6) appropriately evaluates Schumpeter's contribution.

> The source of these two assumptions (added: The assumptions are: (1) growth and progress occurring in spurts and (2) fusion of cycles and growth) is Schumpeter and, in my opinion, it is in his work that we shall find the most fruitful ideas for the analysis of the problem of trend and cycle. He was surely correct in saying

that the essential element in the theory must be the occurrence of revolutionary advances in technique. It is not that Schumpeter is the only one to hold these views—one has only to think of Wicksell or Professor Robertson amongst others—but he has the most fully developed and integrated theory, and it is with his way of thinking that I am most familiar.

According to Goodwin Schumpeter's important idea of fusion of growth and cycle has been side-tracked because of the economists' preoccupation with the Keynesian system, but some speculations by Harrod and the discovery of awkward statistical material have brought the economists at home to realize the fact that Schumpeter's ideas are bound to play a central role.

Ratchet effects have played a significant role in the post-Keynesian theory of consumption such as Dessenberry and Modigliani. The meaning of ratchet effect is that the peak level of income attained so far by the economy prevents its returning to previous trough when a depression occurs. This effect allows growth and cycles to coexist without the assistance of outside trends. This important notion of ratchet is inherent in Schumpeterian system according to Arthur Smithies (1965, p. 42).

The idea of the ratchet is not really a modern discovery. It is inherent in Schumpeter's notion of the role of equilibrium in economic development, first published in 1912. Equilibrium in his system not only constitutes fetters through which entrepreneur must break. But the subsequent process of expansion and adaptation (recession) established equilibrium at a new and higher level. Thus in his system the tendency towards equilibrium represents both a ratchet and a break.

The theoretical and empirical research in the area of production function has substantially been based on Schumpeter's concept of innovation, technological change and shifts in production function. Schumpeterian osmosis in this branch of economics has proven to be enduring V. Ruttan (1971, pp. 75, 76) notes this carefully.

In spite of differences in production function concept, Schumpeter's definition bears a remarkably close resemblance to the definition of technological change currently used by students of productivity and technological change. Compare for example, a recent definition by Solow with the above quotation from Schumpeter... Fellner (1956a, pp. 35-41 and 1956b pp. 195-6) discusses the same concept under the heading of technological-organizational change.

Evidence presented above is weighty enough to prove the point, on the basis of Stigler's criteria, that Schumpeter has been a great original economist. His analysis has opened new and enduring vistas in the economic universe.

Stigler rightly states that a new idea, like a raw diamond, usually is not born perfect; it is fraught with logical inconsistencies and indecisiveness. It has to be polished which comes with aging. Its logical implications unfold as other economists investigate it theoretically and expirically. As usual, Stigler (1965, p. 14) puts it elegantly and precisely.

A new idea does not come forth in its mature scientific form. It contains logical ambiguities or errors; the evidence on which it rests is incomplete or indecisive, and its main domain of applicability is exaggerated in certain directions and overlooked in others. These deficiencies are gradually diminished by peculiar scientific aging process which consists of having the theory "worked over" from many directions by many men.

Both Keynes' and Schumpeter's theories have been passing through the process laid down by Stigler.

In R.C.O. Matthew's (1959, p. 76) view Schumpeter's theory applies remarkably well to those booms—which are many—which are generated and sustained by the developments in areas such as transportation and frontier expansion. According to Matthews, Schumpeter's theory works in such areas because (1) cumulative effects of transportation improvements tend to be extensive, and (2) transport improvements, unlike other technological improvements, serve the entire economy of the area.

Innovations in modern times are more institutionalized than being promoted by a pioneering entrepreneur. Matthews also thinks that the economic and social process of innovation might differ from industry to industry at the same period of time in history.

Economic effects of technological change have been intensively explored and integrated into economic theory in post-Schumpeterian era. According to Murray Brown (1966, p. 73), Schumpeter has been a pioneer in the study of discrete or epochal kind of technological change.

The number of technological epochs is equal to the number of significant changes in the fund of technological knowledge—knowledge that is sufficiently crystallized to be used in designing capital items. There can be no pre-judgement as to the length of the epochs.

This discrete or epochal change in the characteristics of an abstract technology is an aspect of the watershed analysis that was pioneered by Schumpeter.

It can now be stated that with the application of Stigler's criteria of judging the greatness of an economist, Schumpeter very definitely should be regarded as a great economist. This conclusion is further strengthened when Schumpeter's innovative and majestic performance as the author of *History of Economic Analysis* is added.

7 The future – Keynes and Schumpeter

Very early on Schumpeter understood the essence of capitalist reality to be the pulsating dynamic process of evolution which materializes through entrepreneurial innovations. Unlike the mainstream economists, Karl Marx understood, grasped and emphasized the ever evolving economic processes, which form a unique feature of capitalism. Schumpeter (1942, p. 82) laments the fact that the mainstream economic analysis is so blatantly oblivious to the non-stationariness of capitalism. The definite similarity of views concerning this point exists between Schumpeter and Marx. It must be pointed out that Schumpeter understood and stated as early as 1912 in his *The Theory of Economic Development* that in the evolutionary process of economic development, progressive rationalization of attitudes will lead to the decrease of entrepreneurial function in importance.

Therefore the importance of entrepreneur type must diminish just as importance of military commander has already diminished.

Later in his *Capitalism, Socialism and Democracy* Schumpeter has given a thorough analysis and a definite prediction regarding what capitalism will be changing into. Both Keynes and Schumpeter projected future. Keynes has stated that capitalistic order based on individual initiative and freedom if it can be purged of its serious defects such as unemployment and extreme inequalities is definitely worth preserving and must be preserved through judicious and effective government intervention. In today's terminology Keynes would support a mixed economy. But it must be stated forcefully here that he would not support an indiscriminate and counterproductive intervention into the market system.

In Schumpeter's case, he (Schumpeter) realizes the inevitability of change. Despite his comprehension of the dynamics of capitalism and inevitable change it is subject to, in Schumpeter's writing one senses a lament for the passing away of capitalism. First, as pointed out above, Schumpeter is ruefully saying that majority of the economists have failed to understand and appreciate the life-force of capitalism, i.e., the dynamics imparted to capitalism by entrepreneur and his innovations. Second, he (1942, pp. 72-73) very carefully and empirically states that the spectacular improvement in the material standard of living has occurred only because of capitalism and nothing else. In the forthcoming discussion views of Schumpeter and Keynes concerning the future are examined.

Keynes' predictions concerning the future come from his essay entitled "Economic Possibilities for Our Grandchildren." With great clarity Keynes (1931, p. 360) states the purpose of this essay.

My purpose in this essay, however, is not to examine the present or the near future, but to disembarrass myself of shorter views and take wings into future. What can we reasonably expect the level of our economic life to be a hundred years hence? What are the economic possibilities of our grandchildren?

Keynes wrote this essay in 1930. He assures the readers that the talk of the economic decline of Great Britain is just that. He diagnosed that it was not from old age that Britain is suffering but from growing-pains of over-rapid changes which accompany the transition period. Increase in technical efficiency has been much faster which has contributed to the problem of labor absorption. The monetary and banking system has been lagging behind the rapid rate of technological change. He has stated that even though the world is mired in depression at that time, the pessimists who predict violent change will be proven wrong.

According to Keynes, over a long sweep of history, i.e., from two thousand B.C. to the middle of the eighteenth century, the world made an excruciating slow economic progress because of (1) the lack of notable technological progress, and (2) the utter failure of capital accumulation. The infusion of the vast sums of gold from the new world led to the monetization and subsequently to rise of prices and profits in the European economy that initiated and stimulated capital accumulation since sixteenth century. The magical power of the compound rate took over in the sixteenth century and over the following two hundred years enhanced material standard of living of vast proportions according to Keynes.

In the Keynes' view, problem of unemployment was transitory. Discovery of labor-saving devices was faster than finding the new uses for the displaced labor. Keynes's (1931, p. 364) vision of the future is vibrant and brimming with hope.

But this is only a temporary phase of maladjustment. All this means in the long run that making is solving its economic problem. I would predict that the standard of life in progressive countries one hundred years hence will be between four and eight times as high as it is today. There would be nothing surprising in this even in the light of our present knowledge. It would not be foolish to contemplate the possibility of a far greater progress still.

Keynes speculates that the power of science and compound interest will in the long run relieve people of the basic economic problem. Then the question will arise as to how to creatively enjoy leisure and live wisely and agreeably well. Keynes has surmised that mankind, after 100 years from his writing of "Economic Possibilities for our Grandchildren," in 1930, will have solved the economic problem and, at that time, then, the humanity will start honoring those who can teach how to live creatively for the enrichment of life and will have the time to stand and enjoy the beauty around. Keynes (1930, p. 372) expresses this effectively.

We must honor those who can teach us how to pluck the hour and the day virtuously and well, the delightful people who are capable of taking direct enjoyment in things, the lilies of the field who toil not, neither do they spin.

But beware! The time for all this is not yet. For least another 100 years we must pretend ourselves and to everyone that fair is foul and foul is fair; for foul is useful and fair is not. Avarice, usury and precaution must be our gods for a little longer still. For only they can lead us out of the tunnel of economic necessity into daylight.

The act of accumulation must be prolonged for a while according to Keynes and humanity must think of jam tomorrow and never of jam today. There are forty-two years yet to go for Keynes' prophesy to be fulfilled, but, in the meanwhile, the advanced countries have not done badly at all, to say the least. Impressive empirical evidence exists to support the previous statement. Angus Maddison (1987, pp. 649-98) and the World Bank (1983, World Development Report) have amply substantiated the above contention. The growth of industrialized countries from 1950-73 ranges from 3 to 9.4 percent per year. From 1973-84 the above mentioned growth rate has slowed down for most countries, with exception of Germany, Netherland, and U.K.

The impressive increase in the material standard of living has turned out to be a mixed blessing for humanity according to economists such as S.B. Linder and Tibor Scitovsky. To be sure, mankind has not yet learned to appreciate beauty and enjoy culture for their own sake as Keynes would have liked us to. The very titles of Linder and Scitovsky books are highly suggestive such as, *The Harried Leisure Class* and the *Joyless Economy*, respectively.

The conventional wisdom that increased affluence will result in enhanced leisure which will entail blissful tranquillity and harmony in life has proven to be untrue and exactly the opposite has happened according to Linder. Economic theory would predict that with increased income marginal rate of substitution of income for leisure would diminish. In short, leisure would be valued higher (marginally). Linder states that nothing of the kind has happened. Relentless pursuit of higher income and wealth continues at the accelerated pace which makes life more hectic.

Developing upon the embryo of an idea originally thought of by Roy Harrod, Linder has neatly applied the tools of economic analysis to the problem of economic growth and the ever increasing scarcity of time. It must also be pointed out that Linder has broken some new ground in the process, such as consumption requiring time as production does— an idea that has not been appreciated and incorporated into conventional economic analysis. In the light of Keynes's deeply-felt concern regarding the enriching joy of leisure, it would be appropriate to briefly give the pith of Linder's ideas. Supply of time is continuous and non-accumulable. Time lost is lost forever. As far as the demand for time is concerned, consumption requires time as production does, e.g., to enjoy a movie, an opera, one needs time. Increased income due to economic growth creates demand for consumption but consumption requires time. Consequently, demand for time exceeds the supply of time and hence economic laws become applicable to the analysis of time scarcity. In an equilibrium situation, time must be distributed in accordance with the equimarginal principle among the competing uses of time. When economic growth occurs, productivity per hour increases and this leads to the disturbance in equimarginal principle of the allocation of scarce time. To restore equilibrium, yield on time devoted to other activities, including the time devoted to consumption, must be raised. Time in economic growth becomes increasingly scarce but that necessitates an increase in time allocated to all activities and in consequence, economic growth magnifies the scarcity of time.

Scitovsky differs with Linder on the use of leisure time. According to Scitovsky, consumers in industrialized countries, particularly in America, buy time-saving gadgets with the increased income successively, but after having saved the time make no creative use of it and unwittingly end up spending more time on the same activity. In the end, increased income, time-saving gadgets and the increased leisure adds no joy to the totality of human existence and hence Scitovsky calls it the joyless economy. It must be noted though that Scitovsky's book is characteristically well argued with ingenuity and subtlety. It cannot be dealt with in depth here because this work is mainly concerned with its relevance to Keynes's ideas on the future and the use of leisure to enrich human existence.

In summary, fifty years after Keynes' writing concerning the enjoyment of leisure, the art of living and enjoyment of beauty, the ceaseless pursuit of material goods continues. If Linder and Scitovsky can be believed, availability of ample material goods, removal of the worry and insecurity of not having the basic necessities of life and easy access to education have not deepened the culture and enriched the soul and spiritual existence.

As far as Keynes is concerned, the way to the future has to be by expanding individual freedom and not by encumbering it. The single most important message Keynes leaves behind in chapter twenty-four of *General Theory* is that laissez-faire and government action that is necessary to create adequate aggregate demand are not really a simple trade-off as is sometimes expressed today. Deficient effective demand, to use Keynes' phrase, itself leads to the failure of private enterprise which is the energizing dynamo of capitalism. Besides, the wastes of idle resources is what Keynes calls the intolerable public scandal. The essence of the message is that private initiative and public action must be pragmatically harmonized. He calls individualism the most powerful instrument to better the future. It is hard to resist the temptation to quote from *Encyclopaedia Britannica*, (Vol. 6, p. 825) a statement that captures the essence of Keynes.

An intimate of artist, scholar, and politician alike, cultural entrepreneur, gifted teacher, loyal friend and original thinker, this child of the philosophical tradition of Locke, Hume and Mill late in his life expressed as a single regret that he had not drunk more champagne.

Keynes has been severely criticized (by his critics) and praised (by his followers and admirers). When a man is endlessly subjected to the onslaught of criticism, it is obvious that there is something in what that man promulgates and or what he stands for or symbolizes that the critics want to demolish without leaving any traces. This adduces to that person's greatness as it does in the case of Keynes. There are certain noble traits in Keynes' story that even his severest critics cannot deny. As Schumpeter (1951, p. 266) states there were men involved in negotiating peace after World War I who had more or less the same misgivings as Keynes did, but he never spoke out. Keynes was made of different stuff, he resigned and told the world why says Schumpeter. Keynes was passionately interested in the economic betterment of his beloved England and the world. He gave of himself tirelessly and unhesitantly without any regard for his own survival. The world loves a hero such as he, regardless of his faults.

As pointed out earlier Schumpeter's analysis cum prediction of the metamorphosis of capitalism into socialism has not suddenly sprung up from the Great Depression and the new deal. The germ of an idea has been implanted in his *Theory of Economic Development*. As a firm believer in the social process of evolution, Schumpeter has logically reasoned that entrepreneurial function will be obsolete as many feudal institutions and functions had with the rise of capitalism. Schumpeter has had vast and deep knowledge of history in general and feudalism in particular.

Generally in dealing with Schumpeter's analysis of the metamorphosis of capitalism into socialism, it is stated that the very success of capitalism will kill capitalism. As true as it is in the case of Schumpeter, it leaves out the in-depth analysis abundantly enriched by his knowledge and perception of history. Very carefully and systematically he develops his arguments. The main emphasis is on the promulgation of the rational thinking that capitalism fosters. The mode of rational thinking, mathematics and experimental science which, despite the contempt and hostility by scholastic thought, speedily swept scholastic thought away. The same rational thought carried to its logical limits will transform capitalism into socialism according to Schumpeter. The logic of the rational thinking inevitably propels the change.

Schumpeter states that pre-capitalist behavior was also selfish but what distinguishes capitalism is that it epitomizes rationality and adds a new edge to it in intertwined ways. First, with the monetization of the economy, money becomes a powerful tool of cost-profit calculation. This is highly conducive to the enterprise mentality. Second, rational mental habit permeates like a capillary system and it conquers and subjugates man's medical practice, his view of cosmos, his outlook on life, everything including his concepts of beauty, justice and spiritual ambitions. Third, it gives rise to a new class of men called capitalists who are men of strong will. Fourth, capitalist creed rationalizes behavior and ideas and drives out metaphysical and romantic notions. It recreates not only the new modes of attaining ends but the ends themselves.

According to Schumpeter capitalist civilization is inherently rationalistic and anti-heroic as compared to feudalism. Schumpeter characterizes industrial bourgeois as fundamentally pacifist because it perceives the inner (spiritual) and outer world as rational and is steadfastly bent on projecting the morals of private life into international relations. This is highly controversial, and Aldous Huxley (1937, p. 100), for one, has a completely diametric point of view.

> The fact that armaments to a great extent are manufactured by private firms who have a financial interest in selling weapons of war to their own and foreign governments is also a contributory cause of war.

Schumpeter sharply disagrees with the Marxist and neo-Marxist doctrine that war is due solely to economic conflict between the classes. He does not deny the fact that capitalists like to sell arms and make profits; but capitalist combativeness cannot be explained by class conflicts alone. In his view capitalists, like the feudal lords, do not see war-making as their mission. On the basis of the above reasoning, Schumpeter (1942, p. 128-9) proposes a controversial yet interesting hypothesis.

> As a matter fact, the more completely capitalist the structure and attitude of a nation, the more pacifist—and the more prone to count the cost of war—we observe it to be. Owing to the complex nature of every individual pattern, this could be fully brought out only by detailed historical analysis. But the bourgeois attitude to the military (standing armies), the spirit in which and the method by which bourgeois societies wage war, and the readiness with which, in any serious case of prolonged warfare, they submit to non-bourgeois rule are conclusive in themselves. Marxist theory that imperialism is the last stage of capitalist evolution therefore fails quite clearly irrespective of purely economic objections.

At this juncture, it is appropriate to point out Schumpeter's agreement and differences with Marx. Like Marx, he is a determinist particularly in the social and economic sense. Schumpeter (1940, pp. 129-30) expresses this in no uncertain terms.

Things economic and social move by their own momentum and ensuing situations compel individuals and groups to behave in certain ways whatever they may wish to do—not indeed by destroying their freedom of choice but by shaping and choosing mentalities and narrowing the list of possibilities from which to choose. If this is the quintessence of Marxism then we all of us have got to be Marxists.

Schumpeter concurs with Marx on the point that social and economic events have their own unstoppable momentum which unfolds generating a change, though not the way and of the kind Marx predicted. In summary, Schumpeter is in tune with Marx on the point of endless change and social and economic events having a permanent velocity of their own but he categorically is at variance with Marx on the idea and process of material dialectics. Contrary to Marx, the capitalist rationality carried out to its logical end changes the material behavior of people according to Schumpeter. In his view the growth of natural and physical sciences conjugated with the acceleration of scientific and technological progress during the industrial revolution engendered the mentality that created capitalism is inevitably going to annihilate it. It is the inner logic of the process that propels the change. Consequently, it is simplistic to say that according to Schumpeter it is the very success of capitalism that is going to kill it. The very rational thinking that created and natured science, technology and capitalism is going to end capitalism.

Schumpeter's analysis of the actual process of the transformation of capitalism into socialism is well conceived and logically discerned. The entrepreneur who makes capitalism also makes it obsolete. There was a need for him to create new goods, new methods of production, new marketing, new sources of supply and new methods of financing. He perfected the methods of production and has done his job so well that no additional improvement is required. No challenge and job left for him to do. Accordingly, the entrepreneur becomes obsolete—whatever you do not use you loose. Since profit exists only in a dynamic economy as a reward to the entrepreneurial function, there will be no profit. In the Schumpeterian system, interest as return to capital exists only as a tax on profit. Consequently, when profit is zero, interest will be zero. For a while the bourgeois element will live on profit but interest will disappear. With nothing left to innovate as far as production, management, marketing, financing and business in general is concerned, management of industry and trade would be a matter of routine bureaucratic administration. At this time, to paraphrase Schumpeter, socialism of a very sober type would automatically emerge. His use of language is careful and deliberate. By the term 'a very sober type' he wants to emphasize that after having perfected the techniques of production which offers an abundance of goods and services to a near satiety, emergence of socialism would be peaceful, non-violent and almost spontaneous.

The essence of the entrepreneurial function under capitalism, according to Schumpeter, has been getting things done. Single entrepreneur, a Wagnerian hero, in Schumpeter's estimate, who has been the prime mover in facing uncertainty and getting things done, is replaced by a team of organized researchers. At this stage capitalist economy resembles the stationary state and hence there is no uncertainty left to deal with. Because of its rational character and behavior, the capitalist enterprise tends to automatize progress which then accelerates on its own in spite of capitalism. The entrepreneur who created and nurtured capitalism is not needed anymore. The concept of property ownership is diluted. Schumpeter (1942, p. 142) expresses this dramatically.

> The capitalist process, by substituting a mere parcel of shares for the walls and the machines in factory takes the life out of the idea of property. It loosens the grip that once was so strong—the grip in the sense of legal right and the actual ability to do as one pleases with one's own; the grip also in the sense that the holder of the title loses the will to fight, economically, physically, politically, for his factory and his control over it, to die if necessary on its steps.

The right to property is the central concept of capitalism, when the center does not hold, other things tend to fall apart. Evaporation of touchable and perceptible material property eradicates capitalism out of existence, in Schumpeter's view. He predicts that in such a situation, the best of human energy, ingenuity and effort would seek challenges other than economic.

It is important to point out that Schumpeter does not envision his predictions to materialize in their totality in the near future. At the same time in 1942 when he wrote *Capitalism, Socialism and Democracy*, he thought that he could already see palpable effects of technological perfection and complete satisfaction of human wants. The discussion presented here so far has been an attempt to state Schumpeter's analysis of the breakdown of capitalism in its fullness and richness. No effort has been made to examine its relevance in a historical perspective. It is imperative that its congruence to the reality be critically evaluated. The forthcoming articulation proposes to undertake such a task.

One of Schumpeter's predictions concerning mature capitalism is surfeit of production of goods and services. This overabundance of goods and services creates satiety. In terms of Schumpeter's Austrian school of marginal utility, because of the more than ample supply of goods and services marginal utility of goods and services becomes zero or near zero. At such a point, the relentless drive for goods is diluted. Easy availability and access make goods trite. The stronger pursuit and hankering after goods and services which marks the earlier phase of the budding capitalism is slackened. As pointed out earlier, Schumpeter does not specify a chronological date for his prediction to materialize; but at the same time, he categorically states that some of the predictions concerning the gradual transformation of capitalism into a socialism of what he calls "sober type" have begun to materialize. Because of this observation of Schumpeter, it is entirely proper to scrutinize his hypothesis in the light of the current consumption trends.

Examination of the current consumption trends does not lend any support to Schumpeter's contention. Personal savings-ratios for the OECD countries and U.S. have dropped below their historical average. Savings-ratios of West Germany and Japan have not decreased. The *Economist* (March 19, 1988, p. 76) reports the savings-ratios of the above mentioned countries.

Last year the total savings of OECD households dropped below 10% of their disposable income—the lowest savings ratio for a quarter of a century and down from peak of more than 14% in the mid-1970s. America's personal savings ratio has dropped from 8% in 1981 to a 40-year low of below 4% in 1987. Britain's has fallen from 14% in 1980 to just under 6% last year. And in Sweden and Norway personal savings ratios have become negative recently i.e., households are borrowing more than they are saving. On the other hand Japanese and West German households remain as thrifty as ever, their savings ratios have actually risen slightly.

As can be judged from the above, with the exception of West Germany and Japan, the evidence is overwhelmingly against Schumpeter's hypothesis. In fact, in the United States, the burgeoning growth of malls, the world's most extensive interstate highway system with a mall-feeding well-planned network of beltways, loops, bypasses, feeders and interchanges accompanied by the magnetic credit-card system have unleashed consumption of unprecedented proportions. A special supplement to the *Wall Street Journal* (Friday, May 13, 1988, p. 5R) depicts the consumption extravaganza very effectively.

Few envisioned how television's siren song would unleash cravings to be satisfied with the flick of a magnetically coded plastic card, or how malls would proliferate in response.

It would be appropriate to say that Schumpeter's process of creative destruction is very much at work, if not at an accelerated rate. The consumer is endlessly presented with newer goods and gadgets with the ever-easier access to credit. The weight of evidence at this point in time is against Schumpeter's hypothesis of satiation of wants.

Schumpeter has also predicted that under capitalism techniques of production would reach perfection and the happening of which would eliminate the challenge to the entrepreneur. Consequently, entrepreneurial function would become extinct. Schumpeter's contention that production techniques would acquire perfection under capitalism has not yet come true. There also does not seem a possibility of its materializing in the near future. The march of technological advancement is thrusting forward quite rapidly though not at an even pace. The evidence available on this count is weighty enough to refute Schumpeter's contention completely.

Recent empirical investigations concerning the role of technological change and economic growth are systematically reported by Ralph Landau (1988, p. 47).

Based on recently available data and a more sophisticated methodology that prices of capital in relation to its age, Jorgenson states that since World War II capital investment has been responsible for about 40 percent of the growth of the U.S.'s G.D.P. whereas factor productivity accounts for about 30 percent. The remainder can be traced to increase in the quality and quantity of labor. Angus Madison of the University of Groninhgen in the Netherlands has recently reviewed a number of studies on economic growth done in the past 30 years and reaches similar conclusions ... How does investment in capital stimulate productivity to cause economic growth? The answer is found in the way technological change is incorporated into capital. Except for small part devoted to basic science, research and development is seldom undertaken unless its results are expected to be applied in new facilities and superior operating modes that can increase productivity, reduce costs or raise the quality of goods or services.

Other developments in technology as applied to production techniques are also discernible. One such development is flexible manufacturing in which different products are produced by the same capital equipment. It is now common knowledge that computer based technology is applied to production and services at a very brisk pace. Rapid integration of laser-based technology in manufacturing and medicine is another illustration which shows that production techniques have experienced a quantum jump. Rapid advances in automation and telecommunication have also aided further acceleration in production techniques. A distinguishing feature of modern technology is its world-wide spread at an unprecedentedly high rate. This outcome is due to investment abroad undertaken by multinational corporations, international licensing of technology, training and education of an increasing number of scientists and engineers from LDCs in the universities of the West, quicker access to up-to-date knowledge through learned journals, increased global travel and communications. As a result of all the above factors, improvement in production techniques has become a global phenomenon which Schumpeter could never foresee. Production techniques reaching perfection and not requiring further stimulus by entrepreneurs has turned out to be a myopic generalization by Schumpeter.

There is enough evidence to show that Schumpeter's prediction concerning obsolescence of the entrepreneurial function has not proven right. Entrepreneurial function as Schumpeter thought it to be, mainly in getting things done, is very much alive. In other respects, Schumpeter's prediction that, instead of a single struggling innovator, there will be teams of organized and trained researchers by corporations as the major source of innovations in future has been borne out as far as certain industries are concerned. Today both sources of innovation coexist.

In the American economy during the mid-eighties there has been tremendous resurgence of entrepreneurship. The period of the 1970's and early 1980's was dormant as far as innovations and entrepreneurship is concerned. Stagflation and no-growth were the terms applied to express the lack-luster performance of the U.S. economy for above period. But the mid-eighties have changed all that. Sometimes it is believed that this strong resurgence has been mainly due to the emergence of high technology. Embodiment of high tech in areas such as telecommunication, robotics, biogenetics and bioengineering has opened up vistas undreamed of before. As significant as high tech has been in the resurgence of innovations and entrepreneurship, it alone does not account for the total phenomena the American economy is enjoying which were thought to be outside the scope of management. According to Peter Drucker (1985, p. 14), management techniques are being applied to the unconventional and previously untried areas such as small enterprises, nonbusiness enterprises like health care and education, restaurants and even prison management. Drucker (1985, p. 1) summarizes this phenomenon of entrepreneurial rejuvenation appropriately.

Management is the new technology (rather than specific new science or invention) that is making the American economy into an entrepreneurial economy. It is also about to make America into an entrepreneurial society. Indeed, there may be a greater scope in the United States—and in developed societies generally—for social innovation in education, health care, government, and politics than there is in business and the economy. And again, entrepreneurship in society—and it is badly needed—requires above all application of basic concepts, the basic techne' of management to new problems and new opportunities.

Exception could be taken to Drucker's proposition that innovation opportunities have somehow dried up or are less in private business than they are in social, education and government. As long as the flame of human imagination keeps burning, which it always will, opportunities for innovations in the private sector are inexhaustible. For example, as long as diseases such as cancer, arthritis and heart attacks continue to plague humanity, search and research for drugs by private pharmaceutical companies will continue. Since both husband and wife are working full-time, there could be a rapid robotization and automation of household work. Advanced technology such as air-conditioned lawnmowers are not made affordable to the masses yet.

But Drucker's point must be taken seriously. The areas of economic activity or human activity in general which were thought to be immune to innovations have been successfully deimmunized. This invigorated entrepreneurship is not only restricted to the domestic market and traditional U.S. exports but has deeply and widely penetrated the markets abroad. Smaller and midsize companies along with the traditional export giants such as pharmaceuticals have firmly established themselves as robust exporters. *Fortune* magazine of June 6, 1988 reports some unconventional exports from U.S. such as New Hampshire shoes to Italy, Ohio sand to Saudi Arabia, Minnesota chopsticks to Japan and many other products. In essence, all of the above goes to show that in contrast to what Schumpeter predicted the entrepreneurial spirit is alive and doing its thing.

But it must be noted that some of Schumpeter's predictions have fully or at least substantially been borne out. As Schumpeter has foretold, innovations are increasingly institutionalized, i.e., (1) they are carried out by corporations, (2) becoming products of team-work and

(3) requiring coordinated and integrated efforts by various divisions of an organization, i.e., coordinated efforts are required by research and development division and food and beverage division. The last two could be lumped together because they denote team work. But a difference of a sort does exists. Corporations today are organized in divisions. Different divisions are engaged in diverse activities such as household products, and food and beverages. Research and development could be done in a laboratory by a team of highly trained scientists. This is team-work. But when it is necessary to seek help or borrow the work done by other divisions of the same corporation to complete or make the product or process viable, this requires well-coordinated efforts by the various divisions of a corporation. In this sense the last two could be separated. Schumpeter might not have separated the two explicitly the same way as it is done here but his wording such as bureaucratization of innovation, routinization of innovation and team-work certainly connote the meaning as it is expressed above.

Kenneth Labich, (*Fortune*, June, 1988, p. 51) lists the successful innovations introduced by the U.S. corporations.

A list of important products introduced by American companies in just the past five years is breathtaking, ranging from Lotus 1-2-3 software to Chrysler minivans, from Abbot Laboratories' AID antibody test to Apples Macintosh, from Kodak's lithium batteries to Merck's cholestrol-lowering drug, Mevacor. Last year more than 25% of 3M's worldwide sale were generated by products new to the market in the past five years.

This indicates clearly that the epoch-making innovations are created by corporations. According to Kenneth Labich, research and development funds flow freely in innovative companies and scientists are looked upon as a commodity worth investing in for future returns. At GE, research and developmental expenditures have risen 54% since 1982 and the total amounts to $1.2 billion and Johnson and Johnson has spent $617 million on research in 1987 which is about 8% of its sales and was five times the amount spent 10 years ago. According to Kenneth Labich (*Fortune*, June 1988, p. 52) companies, to get the best out of R and D expenditures, try to give commercial incentives to their research teams.

To get the biggest bang for their research bucks, innovative companies go to great lengths to guide their development teams into areas with greatest commercial potential... Most innovative companies provide their scientists with two possible ladders of advancement. They can stay in the lab and move up on the basis of scientific achievement almost as they would in a university. Or they can move into management and head product development teams. When the system is working right, enough researchers choose each path so that good ideas and the people to channel them into specific products bubble to the surface with regularity.

The above analysis adequately substantiates Schumpeter's prediction that research will gravitate more towards team work in the future. This does not in anyway state that the individual innovator is totally extinct. It simply supports Schumpeter's contention that innovations based on the simple knowledge of science are nearly exhausted and the phenomenally accelerated rate of growth of knowledge and research costs, which are beyond the means of a single researcher, necessitate that research and development be undertaken by corporations with adequate resources by organizing teams of highly trained scientists.

As pointed out earlier, innovative companies continually conjugate their various divisions in the process of innovation. Kenneth Labich in the above quoted article expresses this well.

Innovative companies continually bring together the various divisions involved in the product development. These contacts might be informal in the early stages of project... When all the hands are pulling together the process of discovering a product and getting it out can seem almost effortless. Procter and Gamble's recent introduction of calcium-enriched Citrus Hill orange juice showed unusually close coordination between seemingly diverse divisions.

Schumpeter's prediction concerning the bureaucratization of research and development by teams of highly trained scientists, employed by corporations, is adequately substantiated by the evidence presented above.

As a theorist, Schumpeter does not envision the progress of science as a unilinear process in the same direction, but as a continuous crisscross process which though not always logical is yet a manifestation of the inner inclination and spirit of the new contributors. He (1954, p. 4) succinctly expresses this.

Scientific analysis is not simply a logically consistent process that starts with some primitive notions then adds to the stock in a straight-line fashion. It is not simply progressive discovery of an objective reality—as is for example, discovery in the basin of Congo. Rather it is an incessant struggle with creations of our own and our predecessors' minds and it 'progresses', if at all, in a criss-cross fashion, not as logic, but as the impact of new ideas or observations or needs, and also as the bents and temperaments of new men, dictate.

This is an important thought. An exegesis of Schumpeter's view can be put forth in the following way. In economic theory, in Schumpeter's view, the process of evolution has reached its height in Walras, whom he calls the greatest economist so far—that is the time Schumpeter wrote *History of Economic Analysis*. The static problem of allocation of resources under the conditions of perfect competition in which the parametric functions of prices plays a crucial role. Oscar Lange in *On Economic Theory of Socialism* expresses the parametric role of prices in which they (prices) are a resultant of the behavior of all individuals on the market, wherein each individual regards actual market prices as given data to which he has to adjust himself. Each individual tries to exploit the market situation confronting him which he cannot control. Market prices are thus parameters determining the behavior of individuals. Allocation of resources under static competitive general equilibrium process attained its zenith according to Schumpeter.

But the essence of capitalism, which Schumpeter has wanted to explain and has done it par excellence, is the dynamic process of creative destruction whose cause is the innovator. Enough has been said about this aspect in the earlier discussion and hence there is no reason for its repetition. The subject matter under discussion is the end of that process of creative destruction. An abundance of evidence indicates that Schumpeter hypothesized of the end of capitalism and its transformation into socialism too early. Events and economic policies surrounding the Great Depression led Schumpeter to the belief that unfettered capitalism is gone forever. That is why he used the term capitalism in oxygen tent. If there ever was an era of unfettered capitalism or what Kenneth Boulding calls cowboy capitalism, Schumpeter would be right in lamenting the demise of such capitalism.

Entrepreneurial function, which plays such a pivotal role in the system, has not been obsolete or wilting as Schumpeter predicted. John Burch (1986, p. 4) illustrates with examples how the entrepreneurial spirit is very much alive and playing a vital role in the way Schumpeter envisioned.

Today the entrepreneurial beat goes on, played by entrepreneurs such as Eden de Castro, founder of Data General; An Wang, founder of Wang Laboratories; Steven Jobs, cofounder of Apple Computer;

L.J. Sevin, founder of Compaq Computers; and Fred Smith, founder of Federal Express. Literally thousands other successful entrepreneurs could be mentioned. The point is that these people and others like them provide a variety of job opportunities and also serve as role models to inspire new generations of entrepreneurs. Moreover, they have reaped huge rewards for themselves and the venture capitalists who had the foresight to back them.

By all measures, entrepreneurship is stridently thriving and displays no symptoms of being in an oxygen tent. Today's entrepreneurship is spread out and pervasive in all areas of a firm such as production, management, finance, marketing and human relations. Looking at today's luxuriant growth of entrepreneurship, it is evident that Schumpeter has been a victim of myopic vision. It is interesting to point out that part of Schumpeter's argument of the end of capitalism is based on the idea of surfeit of goods and services which he squarely has founded on the law of diminishing marginal utility. When a complement is added to the consumption of a commodity the law of diminishing marginal utility can be temporarily suspended. For example abundance of television sets/programs could be subject to diminishing returns but when a VCR/Beta Max complements the use of television, there is a shift in the utility function.

In terms of input-output analysis, innovations lead to an array of backward and forward linkages. The introduction of personal computers created an enormous market for software, a forward linkage, which tends to be more skilled human capital intensive and could be produced in a garage. The advent of the personal computer also created a huge market for microchips. This is a backward linkage. Finally, a personal computer itself becomes a tool/an input in production, finance and marketing. Evidently, what one sees is an innovation breeding more innovations. Similar situations exist in any new industry, such as biotechnology, telecommunications, robotics and so forth.

As long as the human mind is free to speculate, in a developed society, there will be innovations. Some innovations definitely are in response to a challenge, for example, raising the per gallon mileage of automobiles. Some innovations simply are outcomes of human curiosity. The abounding examples of present innovations clearly show that Schumpeter's fear of the impending arrival of socialism, in the way he predicted, has turned out to be unfounded. Schumpeter's response to such a charge could be that capitalism as it exists today is tamed, softened and interfered with too much by the government. The first part of the answer to Schumpeter would be yes, but tamed capitalism has certainly not stunted the vitality of entrepreneurial growth.

As pointed out earlier, the entrepreneurial beat goes on. The second part would be that the unfettered cowboy capitalism Schumpeter discusses never was. The history of economic policy, especially in the U.S., in terms of laissez-faire vs. state intervention has been controversial and much discussed. William Letwin (1972 pp. xxxii), who has done both an intensive and exhaustive study of the history of economic policy comes to the following conclusion.

What then does the history of economic policy reveal about the theory of theories of economic policy that Americans have entertained? The answer one is forced to is that economic doctrines have never as much influenced the making American economic policy as have political and constitutional considerations. The reason why the whole American economic policy looks so incoherent—with mercantilist, socialist liberal, or autarkic elements all living happily side by side—is that political balance rather than economic consistency have been the more powerful drive.

Koppel Pinson (1966, p. 238), an historian, gives the following account of the German economic policy.

The failure to regulate cartels during Second Reich should not be taken as an expression of laissez faire policy. The tradition of laissez faire in German economic policy was very weak and, except for a brief heyday in the 1885's and 1860's, was soon overshadowed by much more vigorous governmental policy. Reference has been made to the state nationalization of railroads in 1879.

The evidence presented casts a severe doubt over Schumpeter's notion of unfettered capitalism. Most probably, judging from his own model of economic development in which flexible credit creation by banks facilitates innovations, Schumpeter has in mind government allowing big banks to exert strong control over industrial business. In essence, government not only not applying antitrust laws but, if not directly aiding, at least having a benign attitude towards the whole process. This process did not escape from Alfred Marshall's shrewd eye because in his *Industry and Trade* he notes that the German great banks have overstretched and ventured beyond their limits in providing credit to industrial business. In conclusion, Marshall states that each of the great banks has representatives and the representatives of banks have exercised at least for two generations strong control on individual business. To Schumpeter, this represents an inevitable part of the process of innovation and creative destruction. Tampering

with it by taming it would be destroying the very essence of capitalism in his view.

The thread of argument left hanging can be now be woven into the
tapestry of argument. According to Schumpeter (1954, p. 39), the
main business of the analytical economics in the sense of its progress
has always been deepening of the knowledge of competitive price.

This property has been best illustrated by an example: from the
earliest time until today, analytical economists have been interested, more or less, in the analysis of the phenomenon that we call
competitive price.

In Schumpeter's view, as far as this aspect of economic theory is
concerned, Marx stands in splendid isolation as an exception. In no
uncertain terms he assigns credit to Marx for fulfilling this lacuna of
economic theory by working out the evolutionary metamorphosis of
one economic system into another. It might be appropriate to point
out that in this sense Schumpeter's own work, which is the major interest here, parallels that of Marx, and he (Schumpeter) can be considered as a child of Marx. Schumpeter (1954, p. 391) categorically
states the importance of Marx from this point of view.

The other is still more important. Marx's theory is evolutionary in
the sense in which no other economic theory was: it tries to un-
cover the mechanism that, by its mere working and without the
aid of external factors, turns a given state of society into another.

It must be strongly emphasized that the similarity between Marx and
Schumpeter is limited and ends with the metamorphosis of one system
into another. Their visions, preanalytic cognitive acts in Schumpeter's
own nomenclature, are altogether different. As Marx's predictions
have not come true in the case of aging capitalism, so Schumpeter's
have not. On the contrary, what Schumpeter might have thought never
to be reversible has happened. As adequately pointed out earlier,
there has been a strong resurgence of innovations and enterprising
spirit.

From the point of view of economic policy, the Keynesian interventionist policies have been successfully countered by two movements
from the right. One, Milton Friedman has tirelessly espoused the
merits of the market system and in this mission he is ably joined by
George Stigler. Two, James Buchanan and Gordan Tullock have created and successfully promulgated a new discipline of public choice
in economics which points out the futility of government interven-

tion into the market system. Paul Gottfried and Thomas Fleming detail the counter-surge and growth of the conservative movement intellectually and policy-wise in their book, *The Conservative Movement,* published in 1988. Schumpeter would have been happier to see such a rejuvenation of the capitalist system. It goes without saying that there are significant differences between a Schumpeterian system and, Friedman and Buchnan.

A clue to Schumpeter's vision could be found in the general atmosphere prevailing in Germany and Austria during the period of his maturation. Intensive fermentation of ideas in philosophy, natural and social sciences, art and music was occurring in these countries during Schumpeter's formative years. A sensitive and scholarly person such as Schumpeter could not but be deeply affected by the highly charged intellectual atmosphere existing then. A recurring theme in Thomas Mann's novels, particularly in his novel, *Buddenbrooks,* is the softening of bourgeois spirit. According to Thomas Mann the bourgeois values, competence and ethics create capitalist civilization. Without these values capitalist civilization will decline. This in essence is what Schumpeter has hypothesized. In no way does this diminish Schumpeter's contribution to economic analysis and his greatness as an economist.

At this juncture, the time has come to summarize or encapsulate the salient points of the forgone discussion. This has been the study of the two greatest economists of the first-half of the century. Undoubtedly, there are differences between Keynes and Schumpeter. But it is attempted to show that there are certain similarities and affinities of basic theoretical points between them. Keynes moved mountains and reversed the flows of the mighty rivers of classical economics. Regardless of the monetarists counterrevolution, the foundations of macroeconomics laid by Keynes are here to stay. It is proposed here that Schumpeter, at the early stage of his intellectual life, was determined to push economics beyond the static general equilibrium analysis of Walras. As early as 1910 Schumpeter realized and predicted that modern static economic theory would inevitably be Walrasian. Schumpeter (1951, p. 79) forcefully and prophetically states this.

Whoever knows the origin and workings of the exact natural sciences knows also that their great achievements are in method and essence of the same kind as Walras'. To find exact forms for the phenomena whose interdependence is given us by experience, to reduce these forms to, and derive them from, each other: this is what the physicists do, and this is what Walras did. And Walras did it in a new field which could not draw on centuries of preparatory work. He did it immediately with very favorable results.

In *History of Economic Analysis*, Schumpeter devoted twenty-eight quality pages to Walras.

By the same token Schumpeter has found Walras' analysis static, without business cycles, without uncertainty, without credit creation by the banks, without the process of creative destruction and without the activity of innovations and entrepreneurs. Walrasion general equilibrium simultaneous equations may be elegant but there is no entreprepreneur as an agent provocateur. To Schumpeter, the very pith of capitalism consists of the process of innovations and the creator is the innovator. The circular flow is simply an analytical construct to provide a contrast to the dynamic display of capitalist impulses. Schumpeter strived, very successfully, to elevate economic analysis to realistic dynamic heights. For precisely this reason, as pointed out earlier, he found Marx's evolutionary mythology congenial. In this narrow sense, doctrinal lineage between Schumpeter and Marx does exit. Their visions of capitalism are radically different as is clear from the previous analysis.

The Great Depression, the birth of *The General Theory* and entailing subsequent interventionist economic policies transitorily overshadowed Schumpeterian economics. It might be highly appropriate at this point to remember what Schumpeter (1951, p. 76) wrote about Walras in 1910.

Though for a long time Walras did not have defenders, he lived to see the time when he could take pleasure in the knowledge that his ideas needed no defense and that they moved beyond the realm of scientific fashion.

In the heydays of Keynesianism Schumpeter had few defenders. And unfortunately Schumpeter did not live to see the rejuvenation of interest in his economics. Like Walras's ideas, Schumpeter's ideas need no defense and have definitely surpassed the realm of scientific fashion. On this count, no better evidence can be marshaled than the one given by Tobin (1983, p. 455).

Yet from the perspective of the 1970s Johnson viewed Keynes's contribution with much less enthusiasm than in his student days and with less favor than his famous retrospect of 1961, the "General Theory After Twenty Years". Impressed by the post-war performance of capitalism, Johnson concluded that Keynes and Keynesians had over-generalized from the Depression a unique decade in a long history. (Joseph Schumpeter, Harry's Harvard teacher, had said this at the time. In other respects as well, in his unflattering attention to the sociology of politicians and intellectuals, Johnson became Schumpeterian in his later years.)

This is a story of an economist of the caliber and stature of Harry Johnson who has made seminal contributions and has had a solid reputation for his objectivity. Schumpeter has appropriately stressed this over-generalization from the depression by Keynes and his followers. Vigorous economic performance of the world economy during the postwar period and resurgence of innovations and entrepreneurial spirit led Johnson and many other economists to renew their interest in Schumpeter.

The intent and spirit of our study has not been to pit Keynes against Schumpeter. This endeavor has been undertaken with a reverence, though not blindness, for both Keynes and Schumpeter. As stated earlier this study is undertaken to unearth and point out some similarities and differences between these two economists of unique stature that were not explored before.

8 Keynes's theory of probability and induction

This is an attempt to explore the roots of Keynes's beliefs, philosophy and world-view and, possibly, to establish some connection with his economics. *Treatise on Probability*, though not his first book, was the maiden effort of his intellectual prowess. For five years, 1906 to 1911, his intellectual energy was harnessed to the subject of probability. Before discussing his theory of probability, it might be instructive to gauge the power of Keynes's intellectual dynamo. Many economists will readily agree to the fact that Keynes had enormous cerebral power. But testimony from an intellectual giant such as Bertrand Russell (1967, p. 97) lets us fathom the genius-like intellectual capacity of Keynes.

> Keynes's intellect was the sharpest and clearest that I have ever known. When I argued with him, I felt I took my life in my hand, and I seldom emerged without feeling something of a fool. I was sometimes inclined to feel that so much cleverness must be incompatible with depth, but I do not think this feeling was justified.

Keynes was fully aware of the importance of the subject of probability and the fascination that laws of chance present to man's intellectual precociousness. He also knew at that time that such an important field of probability and the logical foundations on which the laws of probability rest was left unharvested for half a century by the mighty intellectuals of Cambridge. Keynes (Keynes, 1973, p. 473) appropriately expresses this.

The list is long; yet there is perhaps, no subject of equal fascination to men's minds on which so little has been written. It is now fifty-five years since Dr. Venn, still an accustomed figure in the streets and courts of Cambridge, first published his *Logic of Chance*, yet amongst systematic works in the English language on the logical foundations of probability my treatise is next to his in chronological order.

Keynes's objective in his theory of probability was to appraise the fundamental process of human reasoning, particularly, to examine the process of induction. In such a process, he was inevitably led to the study of probability because the knowledge acquired by the process of induction does not lead to absolute certainty. Keynes set out to link the abstract theory of probability to the theory of induction, which he thought the earlier probability theorists had not done. He wanted to deduce maximum possible inferences from a minimum number of self-evident axioms in the area of probability and induction as Whitehead and Russell had done with supreme success in the area of mathematics in their *Principia Mathematica*. It should be remembered that Keynes's work, though containing enough mathematical symbols, is mainly concerned with the appraisal of the logical structure of the theory of probability. Roy Harrod, one of Keynes's biographers, thinks that no comprehensive and erudite study of induction has been undertaken since Aristotle, as done by Keynes. Besides being an eminent economist, Roy Harrod has also done significant work in the theory of induction. He (Harrod) admittedly is a friendly critic but his academic and intellectual integrity is of such a high caliber that he cannot be called favorably partial to Keynes.

Keynes's *Treatise on Probability* should be looked upon from the following salient points of view. First, it is a testimony of Keynes's mental powers and logical faculty. It is a display of his ability in distinguishing the finest nuances of apparently and seemingly identical propositions and logical relations. It demonstrates his ability in delving into unparalleled depths and delicately revealing the subtleties of the arguments involved. As pointed out earlier, its main thrust is not in working out the mathematics of theory of probability. It is a first and superb effort in establishing and delineating the links in the chains of reasoning from intuitive perceptions to induction by the route of probability.

Second, Keynes's mathematical ability should be studied from a special point of view. The ability referred to is different from simply doing the pedestrian mathematics of probability. Specifically, under discussion is the same type of mathematical ability as displayed by Whitehead and Russell, that is, the ability to draw maximum inferences on the basis of minimum self-evident axioms. In *Principia Mathematica*, Russell and Whitehead developed a system of logic out of which mathematics was to be generated. According to Roy Harrod, in all probability in England at that time there were only two persons who were adept in the kind of logic Keynes employed in his theory of probability and both of them rated Keynes's work very highly.

Third, upon reading Keynes's *Treatise on Probability* it indicates that he had developed enormous scholarship in the history of thought. It is true that Keynes was dealing only with a certain aspect of the theory of probability and possibly could not write a survey of the development of theory of probability. He uses those sources of historical development that were central and relevant to the problem at hand.

Finally, it is indicative of Keynes's capacity of theorization on the basis of abstract principles. It illustrates his view concerning assumptions of a theory, theory itself and applicability of conclusions of a theory. An effort will be made later on to see the relevance in Keynes's beliefs in general and his theory of probability. As noted by his students his sense of realism was unsurpassed compared to other contemporary economists. He possessed a third eye which was habitually known to have been looking below the surface.

Instead of talking around Keynes's theory of probability, the time has come to go to the very heart of it. According to Keynes human knowledge is acquired by two methods: part of it is acquired by direct observation and part by argument. The theory of probability deals with that part of knowledge which is acquired by argument in degrees from the point of view of conclusiveness or inconclusiveness. Keynes's concept of probability is not subjective. To him a proposition becomes probable when the facts on which it is said to be probable are objectively and independently judged. The theory of probability is logical because it is determined independently of the subjective beliefs of certain people. It is also logical because it deals with the degree of belief which is rational to hold under a given set of circumstances. In other words, a proposition is conditionally probable in terms of degrees, wherein the conditions are deemed to be rational objectively and independently. The same theory can be used to draw logical inferences on the basis of the premises that are based on direct knowledge. In Keynes's view conclusions based on probabilistic inference should not be called uncertain or doubtful. Instead, they strictly ought to be expressed in the degrees of rational belief.

Keynes's views are opposed to the frequency theory of probability, namely the measurement of probabilities, in the sense that according to him probabilities in general are not measurable. This aspect of his theory of probability also has an important bearing on his view concerning econometrics. It is well known to economists that Keynes never gave his blessing to econometrics, much to the dismay of many econometricians. According to him probabilities are also not comparable in the sense that it cannot be said that probabilities are greater than, equal to or less than each other. To him to say that probabilities are measurable is to assume that they can be placed in an order of magnitude. He thinks that more attention has been given to the calculus of probability than to the logical foundation upon which its superstructure is created. He (1973, 1921, p. 22) lucidly explains this.

The calculus of probability has received far more attention than its logic, and mathematicians, under no compulsion to deal with the whole of the subject, have naturally confined their attention to those special cases, the existence of which will be demonstrated at a later stage, where algebraical representation is possible. Probability has become associated, therefore, in the minds of theorists with those problems in which we are presented with a number of exclusive and exhaustive alternatives of equal probability; and the principles, which are readily applicable in such circumstances, have been supposed, without much further enquiry to possess general validity.

Keynes also objects to the induction or generalization that is done on the basis of repeated experiments, particularly the notion that increased instances add to the probability of generalization. He sees no rationale in attributing a numerical measure to the increase. In his view there are four alternatives. First, in some cases there is no probability at all. Second, there are cases in which probabilities do not all belong to a single set of magnitudes measurable in terms of a common unit. Third, in some cases measures might always exist, but in many cases they must remain unknown. Fourth, there are cases in which their measures are capable of being determined by us, but we are not always able to determine them in practice. A limited class of probabilities are measurable according to Keynes and a common unit of measurement for such probabilities could possibly be found, but the difference between the probabilities that are measurable and those that are nonmeasurable is not fundamental in his view.

Keynes does not want to deal with the partial or narrow definition of probabilities by restricting it only to the category of measurable probabilities. At this point, it would be appropriate to paraphrase his view. He says that he is totally averse to limit the scope of the word probability and would very much prefer to use it in its widest sense. He is fully aware of the fact that his proposition that not all probabilities are measurable seems paradoxical but that is due to the current use to which the term probability is put by the adherents of the frequency theory of probability. Those who use the measurable definition of probability in general are not aware of the inconsistency involved in their view because, in doing so, they excluded the probabilities that are not measurable. Probability theorists who call the nonmeasurable probabilities as unknown probabilities are simply dodging the intricate problem definition. But to him it is indicative of the fact that the current and widely used relative frequency definition of probability is too narrow or partial.

Some of the main properties of Keynes's ordered series of probabilities can be expressed in the following way: (1) every probability is situated on a path between the two extremes of certainty and impossibility. A degree of probability is never identical with certainty or with impossibility. From this it follows that certainty, impossibility and a degree of probability between them are ordered series. This also implies that every proposition can be proven, disproven or can be assigned an intermediate position, (2) density or compactness is not a characteristic of a path composed of probability. In Keynes's view, it is not necessarily true that any pair of probabilities in the same series have a probability between them, (3) the same degree of probability can lie on multipaths. This means that the same degree of probability can belong to multiseries and (4) in the case of ordered series transitivity condition is satisfied, that is, if ABC form an ordered series, B lying between A and C, and BCD forms an ordered series, C lying between B and D, then ABCD forms an ordered series in which B lies between A and D.

The above ideas can be depicted on a diagram which is borrowed from Keynes. Different series of probabilities and relations in between and among them are pictured in the diagram below. These are ordered series and all the points on a given path belong to the same series. In accordance with (1), points O and I represent impossibility and certainty respectively. And all paths depicted lie entirely between these two points. In accordance with (3), the same point can occupy more than one path consequently, it is possible for paths to intersect and cross. In accordance with (4), the probability represented by a given point is greater than that represented by any other point which can be reached by passing along a path with a motion constantly towards the point of impossibility and less than that is represented by any point which can be reached by moving along a path towards a point of certainty.

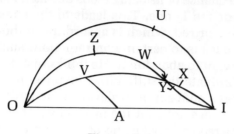

Figure 8.1

O represents impossibility, I certainty and A a numerically measurable probability intermediate between O and I. U, V, W, X, Y, and Z represent non-numerical probabilities. As can be seen, V is numerically less than A, W, X and Y. X and Y are both greater than W and greater than V. X an Y are not comparable with one another or with A. V and Z are less than W, X and Y, but they are not comparable with one another. U is not comparable with any of the probabilities represented in a diagram. Numerically comparable probabilities will all belong to one series called the numerical path or strand. Such a numerical strand or path is OAI in the above diagram.

As we have seen, according to Keynes direct knowledge of probability propositions is necessary. In an effort towards obtaining such a knowledge, he critically examines the principle of non-sufficient reason which he emends and renames as the principle of indifference. He finds James Bernoulli's principle of non-sufficient reason clumsy, unsatisfactory and worth abandoning in favor of the principle of indifference. He (1921, 1973, p. 45) states the principle of indifference in the following way.

The principle of indifference asserts that if there is no unknown reason for predicating our subject one rather than another of several alternatives, then relatively to such knowledge the assertions of each of these alternatives have an equal probability. Thus equal probabilities must be assigned to each of several arguments, if there is an absence of positive ground for assigning unequal one.

Roughly Keynes's principle of indifference means that if there are no reasons for the preference for one rather than another of the available alternatives, then they all have equal probabilities. Application of this principle in its present form creates contradictions. Assume that nothing is known about the color of a certain ball, then chances of its being blue or not blue are equal, that is, each has a chance of one-half. Similarly, the chance of its being red is one-half. Hence the chance of its being blue or red is one. This leads to the conclusion that all balls are either blue or red, which is absurd. Even though the principle of indifference leads to certain contradictions such as the above, Keynes does not want to abandon it. He thinks that it can be properly stated so as to eliminate the difficulties involved for it to be useful. For this, he creates a concept of irrelevance. According to Keynes, if the added premise does not alter the probability, then it is irrelevant. If the color of a person's hair has no bearing on his having a dental problem, the color of hair, then, is an added premise which does not affect the probability of a person's dental malady.

After the above emendation, Keynes's principle of indifference is recast in the following way: The probabilities of x and y relative to given evidence are equal if there is no relevant evidence pertaining to x without corresponding evidence pertaining to y, that is, the probabilities of x and y relative to the evidence are equal, should the evidence be symmetrical with respect to x and y.

Keynes, still, is not out of the woods. One important proviso needs to be added. He excludes those cases, in which one of the alternatives involved is itself a disjunction of sub-alternatives of the same form. When this condition is satisfied, the alternatives are called indivisible relative to the evidence. The following is Keynes's formal definition of divisible. An alternative o(x) is divisible, relative to evidence h, if, given h, o(x) is equivalent to o(y) or o(z), where o(y) and o(z) are incompatible, but each possible, when h is true. It is necessary, here, that o(x), o(y), o(z) values belong to the same propositional function.

Keynes is finally ready to accept as an axiom the principle that, on given evidence, o(x) and o(y) are equally probable on the following conditions: (1) The evidence is symmetrical with respect to x and y, and (2) relative to the evidence, o(x) and o(y) are indivisible.

Keynes's theory of probability has been subjected to criticism which needs to be scrutinized. Before dealing with the criticism of Keynes, it would be highly appropriate to keep in perspective that the subject of probability is vast, many faceted and is asked to perform many tasks that could be contradictory. None of the theories of probability are satisfactory on all grounds. Max Black (1967, p. 477) has ably condensed the scope and task of the probability theory.

None of the chief types of interpretations of probability now in favor can be accepted as wholly satisfactory. One reason may be that an acceptable philosophy of probability is called upon to perform a number of tasks that are hard to reconcile: to show why some probability judgments are a priori while others are contingent, to provide a firm basis for a calculus of probability while recognizing probability judgments that are incorrigibly imprecise, to account for and to defend the connection between rationality and specifiable degrees of confidence in conclusions following with probability from given premises; and above all, to show how and why it is justifiable to act on probabilities.

The above quotation indicates how nearly impossible, if not totally impossible, it is to define probability which will wholly satisfy all the above criteria. Keynes's or any other theory of probability ought to be judged in the light of the above considerations.

Now the time has come in the discourse to deal with criticism leveled at Keynes's theory of probability. According to Bertrand Russell (1948) Keynes's theory requires direct knowledge of probability relations which is impossible. In Russell's view nothing but tautologies can be known independently of experience and Keynes, certainly, will not agree to saying that his probability relations are tautologies. Russell himself mollifies his criticism by saying all the knowledge in the world cannot be empirical and for the empirical knowledge itself to initiate and proceed some direct knowledge, deductive knowledge, is necessary. He thinks that Keynes's requirement of direct knowledge might create certain reticence in accepting Keynes's theory, but it is in itself is not enough of a reason to reject it.

The chief formal defect in Keynes's theory according to Russell consists in treating probability as a relation between propositions instead of between propositional functions. If we are right in interpreting Russell, he wants to separate the propositions from the functions they are supposed to carry out. Apart from the sentence structure and grammar, the propositions are also instruments to convey or carry out certain functions. Propositions appear to apply to individual cases but always to be construed as a judgment about some class of which the individual is a member. Contradictory results are obtained when application is done to an individual. For example, probability of life expectancy of individual x as a Vietnam veteran is different from the life expectancy of x as a member of the class of physicians or as a member of Methodists or as a member of nonsmokers and nondrinkers. Another interpretation, complimentary to the above interpretation, could be a mathematical one. In this case, there could be two variables m (demand for travel) and n (disposable income), wherein m is a dependent and n is an independent variable and could be expressed as

$$m = f(n)$$

But, then, the problem that crops up here is that the whole system becomes deductive, which, as stated above, would be palatable to Russell but of Keynes we cannot be sure.

Braithwaite (1973, p. xvii) objects to Keynes's claim that his theory is applicable to every field in which the term is used. Braithwaite believes that Keynes cogently refuted the claim of a frequency theory that does provide a logic of partial belief. According to him a frequency theory might not adequately explain the rational belief in Keynes's sense, but that does not show that it cannot explain the probabilities which occur within scientific statements such as the probability of a radium atom disintegrating within 1622 years is one-half. This example is borrowed from Braithwaite. These propositions are empirically well established and present insurmountable difficulties to Keynes. In Braithwaite's view, since the 1925 statistical laws of quantum physics are so well established they are regarded as empirical generalizations. It must be remembered that Braithwaite is talking here only of the empirical laws of physical sciences. Consequently, the same cannot be attributed necessarily and uncritically to social sciences.

In depth and extensive discussion of Keynes's probability theory is given above for the following three reasons: (1) The probability revolution has impacted upon the natural as well as the social sciences. Keynes's role in that probability revolution needs to be assessed, (2) Keynes has steadfastly refused to do econometrics. He did not endorse any of the efforts done at that time. This has become a very sore point with the leading econometricians and therefore this subject deserves to be investigated with all seriousness and in depth, and (3) this subject inevitably involves us in the subject of causality in economics.

It must be understood that the above three factors are inseparably intermixed.

It might be important at the outset to point out that Keynes thought of economics in wider sense as a branch of humanities, in which theoretical and factual knowledge, strong intuitive imagination and practical judgment are intricately blended in a comfortable zone of human mind. Keynes (1972, p. 335) ably states his views in an obituary to Frank Ramsay.

> ...for the delightful paths of our own most agreeable branch of the moral sciences, in which theory and fact, intuitive imagination and practical judgement are blended in a manner comfortable to the human intellect.

As can be seen, Keynes was not averse to using theory and facts, but in his view unalloyed facts most of the time tend to be imprecise. A mixture of logic and intuition are required to be deployed in the economic interpretation of facts. In his essay on Marshall, Keynes clearly states that it is easy to express the formal economic theory in terms of algebra and differential calculus. Compared to this, what Keynes thought to be extremely difficult was the economic interpretation of complex and incompletely known facts that are not very helpful in establishing meaningful results.

The above discussion concerning Keynes's theory of probability and his views concerning quantitative economics set the tone for the forthcoming discourse. As far as the integration of economic theory with the probability theory is concerned, one cannot help wondering about the fact that some of the most prominent economists of the nineteenth and early twentieth centuries, such as Cournot, Jevons, Edworth and Keynes, have also been the equally prominent contributors to the probability theory. None of the economists mentioned above have contemplated the marriage of economics and probability theory. It also should not be forgotten that Schumpeter and Frank Knight made a finer distinction between risk and uncertainty respectively in 1912 and 1921. There is more discussion concerning the treatment of risk and uncertainty by Schumpeter and Knight at other places.

According to Mary Morgan (1987, p. 135), even though the application of statistics to the measurement and discovery of economic relationships had begun in the late nineteenth century, economists rejected the use of probability mathematics because it was thought to be inapplicable to economic data. By the standards of 1838 Cournot was a well trained probabilist and was fully convinced that the economic theory needed to be reformulated in mathematical terms. The result of Cournot's familiarity with probability did not result in the happy, or unhappy for that matter, marriage of economics and probability theory. In fact his book, *Researches into Mathematical Principles of the Theory of Wealth*, turned out to be a rejection of the idea of applying probability to the core of economic theory. On the contrary, he was inspired by the physicists such as Boltzmann and Gibbs and considered physics the science to be followed.

Cournot played a major role in the mathematization of economics, but probability did not play a central, if any, role in it. This could not be attributed to the underdeveloped state of probability mathematics which was adequately developed. This is because Cournot, who wanted to create rational economics, wanted to follow rational mechanics. The law of profit maximization was thought to be a counterpart of the law of machines. In an article written by Edgeworth and published in the *Economic Journal* (1910), entitled "Applications of Probability to Economics", there is no probability. Of course, Cournot, Edgeworth and Jevons did their work on probability before Keynes.

The above extensive discussion of Keynes's theory of probability has shown that he was not favorably disposed towards the application of probability to the economic theory. Claude Menard (1987, p. 143) has an interesting statement that needs to be commented on.

> But, as was true for Cournot, there is no place in Keynes's economic model for a probabilistic approach. We must go so far as to say, and this is clear in Keynes's correspondence, that he did not think mathematical probability could be a useful tool for economists.

As far as nonapplication of mathematical probability to economic theory is concerned, Keynes and Cournot concur. But unlike Cournot, Keynes has never favored the casting of economic theory purely in mathematical terms. It was at Roy Harrod's insistence, Keynes inserted a diagram in *The General Theory*. The above quote from Keynes's essay on Frank Ramsay does forcefully bring the point home that Keynes did not favor an economics full of algebra and differential calculus.

Trygve Haavelmo's paper "The Probability Approach to Econometrics" published in *Econometria 12* (1944) was the first systematic effort in integrating probability theory in economic measurement. He realized that the majority of econometricians thought that probability theory proper had nothing to offer, though they employed the statistical methods founded on that probability theory. He reasoned that since probability theory was the foundation on which the structure of statistical methods was erected, it was illegitimate to use the one without using the other. Haavelmo cogently expresses his views in the above mentioned work.

> The method of econometric research aims, essentially, at a conjunction of economic theory and actual measurements, using the theory and technique of statistical inference as a bridge pier. But the bridge itself was never completely built. So far, the common procedure has been, first to construct an economic theory involving exact functional relationships, then, to compare this theory with some actual measurement, and finally, "to judge" whether the correspondence is good or bad. Tools of statistical inference have been introduced, in some degree, to support such judgements, e.g., the calculation of a few standard errors and multiple-correlation coefficients. The application of such simple "statistics" has been considered legitimate, while, at the same time, the adoption of defi-

nite probability models has been deemed a crime in economic research, a violation of the very nature of economic data.

As can be sensed, Haavelmo uses rather strong language to express his dissatisfaction. Instead of using simple statistical methods to test the deterministic economic theory, Haavelmo would have economic variables be expressed in stochastic terms. The problems of lack of independence of observations and the lack of homogeneous time periods were the arguments put up by the antiprobability economists. It was thought by the antiprobability economists that the probability logic is only applicable to those series of observations which may be considered as an independent drawing from one and the same population. From this it was inferred that most economic time series do not conform well to any probability model because the successive observations are not independent. In the above cited work Haavelmo answered this charge by stating that it is not necessary that the observations be independent and that they should follow the same one-dimensional probability law. According to him it is sufficient to assume that the whole set of, say, n observations may be considered as one observation of n variables (or a sample point) follow n-dimensional joint probability law, the existence of which may be purely hypothetical. Then, he maintains that a hypotheses could be tested concerning this joint probability law and inferences be drawn by means of one sample point (in n dimensions).

From the point of view of antiprobability economists, the real lacuna, if the theory were cast in probabilistic terms, it seemed that passive observation of reality resulted in data that were time related from changing conditions. In Haavelmo's view, the qualities of independence and randomness can be associated not only with individual observations on individual variables but also with observations on a system of variables $X_1, ..., X_r$. If this were a set of variables thought to influence members of a consuming population; each person's set of variables could be represented by one point in-r-dimensional space and the X would be subject to a joint probability law. To him, probabilistic formulation of economic theory imposed a formal relationship between nonexperimentally obtained data and the theory, which enabled the theory to be tested and therefore economists should think of all economic variables as probability determined. On what foundations could such a belief rest? Discussion concerning the nature and foundations of the theory of probability are futile in his views because they deal with the concept of probability that is abstract. The germane question in his view is not whether probabilities exist or not, but whether— if we proceeded as if they existed—they enable us to make statements about real phenomena that are correct for practical purposes.

Considerable digression has occurred from Keynes's theory of probability and its significance. It must be realized, though, that Haavelmo's was the major effort that, at least, partially frutified. In the same context, it must be mentioned that Haavelmo put up a valiant defense of Tinbergen against Keynes's criticism of Tinbergen's work on business cycles. Tinbergen's was a maiden effort in applying statistical techniques in measuring and testing business cycle. It cannot be denied that Haavelmo conjugated statistical analysis and probability theory. In this sense, he has created a revolution because, since then no econometrician believed in the duality, as older econometricians did, of statistics and probability. Stochastification of the economic theory has not happened as Haavelmo wanted. In this sense it has not created a revolution.

As far as his probability theory is concerned Keynes is supported by an authority of no less stature than Sir John Hicks (1979, p. 105).

> I have myself come to the view that the frequency theory, though it is thoroughly at home in many of the natural sciences, is not wide enough for economics. Indeed, on those points where Keynes and Jeffreys appear to differ, I generally find myself on the side of Keynes.

Hicks's objection to the frequency theory is simple yet subtle. Characteristically Hicks starts with a simple argument concerning definition of probability according to the frequency theory, but before the reader realizes, he is in deep water up to his neck. The definition requires exact repetition of an experiment. If the repetition were exact, outcome must be the same each time. But this is not the import of the argument of the frequency theorists, i.e., the repetitions must not be exact; they must be different in same way, yet they must be repetitions. They must be performed in accordance with the principle of randomness. What is the meaning of random? A sampling is called random when every member of the population has an equal chance (probability) of being selected. Hick's objection to this definition is that every definition of randomness involves some kind of probability. According to Hicks (1979, p. 106) this definition is circular.

> What is meant by random? No one, to my knowledge has given a definition of random which does not refer back to some form of the above definition of probability. So it is not easy to escape the reproach of circularity; if randomness and probability can only be defined, each in terms of other, each is left undefined. There is no way out except to say that we do recognize, empirically, series of trials that do not repeat exactly, which do appear to have the prop-

erty that is expressed in the definition quoted. That such series exist, and are of the greatest importance, is beyond question, but if the basis of the theory is just this empirical recognition, we have no right to assume, without careful examination, that any series we choose to take will fit into that mould.

Hick's objection is fundamental and is not answered by Haavelmo's joint probability estimation because probability itself is left undefined. One also has to agree with Hicks on the point that the frequency definition of probability fails to apply in predicting probability events such as the third world war because these events are not a matter of trials that could be repeated.

Hicks also strikes at the very root of the frequency theory, especially in the context of events in which it is applied. In his view probability is definitely involved in economics, e.g., investments are undertaken and securities are brought and sold on a judgment of probabilities. Both economic theory and economic behavior involve probability. Kind of probability used by economists in the instances such as portfolio theory are not suited to be interpreted in terms of random experiments. Hicks thinks that the concept of probability to be used in economic events and decisions must be wider than cannoted by the frequency theory of probability.

As far as the intellectual position on probability is concerned, Hicks concurs fully with Keynes. It is and always will remain a subject of curiosity and discussion among economists so far Keynes's unwelcome to mathematical economics and econometrics goes. Keynes was hostile to mathematical economics because he considered economics to be basically a branch of humanity and moral science. At Keynes's time econometrics was a budding discipline whose potentialities were highly expected but not fully realized. Despite Keynes's hostility and in spite of his dominance as an economist, a lot of econometrics has been done. After little more than half a century and with a substantial knowledge of econometric theory and applied econometrics, Hicks has reached a verdict concerning the vast enterprise of econometrics that is not very complementary and assuring. Hicks (1979, p. 121) states his negative evaluation in unmistakable terms.

I am bold enough to conclude, from these considerations that the usefulness of 'statistical' or 'stochastic' methods in economics is a good deal less than is now conventionally supposed. We have no business to turn to them automatically, we should always ask ourselves, before we apply them, whether they are appropriate to the problem in hand. Very often they are not. Thus it is not at all sensible to take a small number of observations, (sometimes no more than a dozen observations) and to use the rules of probability theory to deduce from them a 'significant' general law.

Interestingly enough, Schumpeter would have agreed with both Hicks and Keynes on the point under discussion. According to Haberler (1951) Schumpeter was reticent to convert his theory into a mathematical model. Haberler reports that Schumpeter was not very pleased with Frisch's model of his theory which Frisch developed in "Propagation Problems and Impulse Problems in Dynamic Economics." This article of Frisch was published in a book, *Economic Essays in Honor of Gustav Cassel*, in 1933. Haberler believes that Schumpeter would have agreed with Keynes, as far as the dynamic theory is concerned, that in ordinary discourse we can keep at back of our heads the necessary reserves and qualifications and adjustment which we shall have to make later on, in a way in which we cannot keep complicated partial differentials at the back of several pages of algebra. Schumpeter was of the divided mind though. On the one hand he loved the mathematical precision and was enthusiastic about mathematical ingenuity. On the other hand he was troubled about the lack of judgment, ignorance about the intricacies and complexities of the real world on the part of econometricians. Haberler comes to the conclusion that due to post-Keynesian developments in quantitative economics, Schumpeter would have fully agreed with the following remarks of Keynes (1936, p. 298) on this subject matter.

Too large a proportion of recent mathematical economics are mere concoctions, as imprecise as initial assumptions they rest on, which allow the author to lose sight of complexities and interdependencies of the real world in a maze of pretentious and unhelpful symbols.

Irving Fisher played a seminal role in the development of the theory and technique of index numbers. He was very much in favor of using index numbers as a measure of purchasing power of money. But Robert A. Horvath (1987, p. 164) states that Fisher was skeptical and opposed to the use of least square methods in economic measurement because, he thought, characteristics of the data may vary inversely as their deviation (or as its square) from any normal.

Despite the criticism and the real or alleged shortcomings of econometric methods, measurement will continue. It cannot be denied that some economic phenomena are expressed in quantities and hence lend themselves easily to be tinkered with by the econometricians.

There are further serious objections raised by Frank Knight. Econometricians claim that the ultimate aim of their craft is to predict.

An integral part of the theory of probability is Keynes's views on induction. Keynes divides the process of induction in two parts (1) depends on the method of analogy and (2) depends on pure induction. By pure induction he means that part of the argument which arises out of the repetition of instances. He also defines the term negative analogy. This term involves the principle of varying those of the characteristics of the instances, which are regarded in the conditions of generalization as non-essential. On the other hand, positive analogies refer to the principle of varying those of the characteristics of the instances, which are regarded in the conditions of generalization as essential. Probability of any empirical argument depends on the positive and negative analogies and the scope of generalization.

Two kinds of generalizations arise out of empirical argument. The first is universal induction which is more applicable to exact sciences. These generalizations claim universality and a single exception tends to weaken them. The other kind of induction according to Keynes leads up to the laws upon which we can generally depend, but which does not claim, however firmly established, to be a law of more than probable connection. Keynes calls this inductive correlation. At a particular point in time, an inductive argument does not establish a fact to be so, but indicates that in relation to the evidence the probability is in its favor. The validity of a past proposition based on the then evidence is not upset if the truth turns out to be otherwise today.

In Keynes's view Hume's generalizations have come out stronger in probabilistic terms because Hume failed to take into consideration the full import of side conditions in relation to major propositions. It is clear from the discussion on induction that, Keynes must have been determined to examine the fundamental relationship between induction and probability. It is for this reason that some of the initial propositions laid down by Keynes have the character of being too obvious. He has taken that treacherous step from the obvious and simple with supreme skill. Like Hume, Keynes maintains that some degree of resemblance must exist between the various instances upon which generalization is formulated. Instances must belong to the proposition on which it is generalized. Analogy, in some way, must become a part of the process of induction.

As far as pure induction is concerned, Keynes thinks that Hume's argument was tightly reasoned. The object of multiplying the instances is that we are mostly aware of some differences of inter-instances even though it is imperfectly known that the existing differences are of insignificant character and there may be more differences of the same character. Additional instance may diminish the unessential resemblances between the instances and realization of new difference might increase negative analogy. The possibility of this makes new instances highly valuable. This process of repeated instances is essential in the process of induction, particularly in the process of pure induction. Keynes has attached a great significance to these varying, though insignificant conditions, in induction. He states that generalizations of the Newtonian theory and the implications that follow are fulfilled under the circumstances that differ widely from one to another. It is the variety of circumstances under which the Newtonian predictions are realized makes our belief stronger in that system.

According to Keynes, the objective of induction is always to increase negative analogy or to diminish the characteristics common to all examined instances. This can be done by (1) increasing the definite knowledge of instances examined already, and (2) searching for additional instances of which definite knowledge can be obtained. Advanced scientific method relies on the first; crude unregulated induction based on ordinary experience depends on the second. Keynes arrives at a generalization that pure induction does not extend substantial help in solving the problem of general induction.

Requirement of the prior probability for pure induction reduces its potency as a tool of generalization according to Keynes. He takes Jevons to task for not realizing this crucial point. He (1973, p. 265) expresses this in the following terms.

> To take an example, pure induction can be used to support the generalization that the sun will rise every morning for the next million years, provided that with experience we have actually had there are finite probabilities, however small, derived from other source, first in favor of generalization, and, second, in favor of the sun's not rising tomorrow assuming the generalization to be false. ...Those supposed proofs of the inductive principle, which are based openly or implicitly on an argument in inverse probability, are all vitiated by unjustifiable assumptions relating to the magnitude of a prior probability o. Jevons, for instance, avowedly assumes that we may, in the absence of special information, suppose any unexamined hypothesis to be likely as not. It is difficult to see how a belief, if even its most immediate implications had been properly apprehended, could have remained plausible to a mind of so sound practical judgement as his.

Induction depends on the prior presumption that a proposition has an appearance of being true and, in absence of the contrary evidence, of its being true. Sometimes what appears to be true might be false. Even for a probable knowledge, substantial probability relationship is required between what appears to be initially true and in generalization finally turns out to be true. Without the initial a priori knowledge, probable knowledge is not possible in his view.

The question now is what is left of induction and probability based on it. Inductive argument ought to be supported on other grounds than the number of instances upon which they are based, i.e., pure induction. Crucial in induction, according to Keynes, is the degree in which the circumstances of past experiences resemble the known circumstances in which the prediction is to be materialized. In scientific method it is important to search for the means of enhancing the known analogy so that pure induction might be of relatively less importance. When the existing knowledge is sound and the analogy is good, pure induction is relegated to the subservient role. But when the existing knowledge is limited, induction might be the only resort left. In a highly advanced science it is a last alternative. But in a primitive stage of inquiry, pure induction might be the only recourse.

Keynes expresses certain thoughts on epistemology that are highly relevant in evaluating his views and actual theorization. Insufficient beliefs that are based on direct inspection should be regarded significant in epistemology. Development in metaphysics has been greatly obstructed by the insistence on demonstrative certainty. Much of Hume's criticism was directed at that demand for demonstrative certainty. The realists might have reaped more at the end had they been satisfied with lesser initially. This, at least, part has given rise to the transcendental philosophy. Probable knowledge should be considered as real. Instead of an insistence on demonstrative method, new method of taking account of circumstances which seem to provide some reason for choosing one alternative over another.

Keynes's views concerning the development in metaphysics, in this author's view, are applicable to his view and practice in economic theorizing. As pointed out earlier, he regards economics essentially as a moral science. If this is so, which it is, then demonstrative certainty cannot be expected. It would be much more fruitful for the economists to advance argument by taking account of circumstances which seem to present a menu for choice. With demonstrative certainty not being pursued, economists could concentrate on circumstances such as leading to involuntary unemployment which is not postulated according to the Say's law. Would general wage reduction, if the unions would let it happen and given the presence of real balance effect, in a depression restore the economy to full employment? Even before the depression, Keynes's strong and unmistakable orientation towards policy is well known. Examining the circumstances that give rise to a particular situation in order to provide a remedy was his inclination. Such an inclination also is reflected in his views on epistemology. Not being doctrinaire and flexible use of sound and well reasoned judgment has always been the hallmark of his economic policy. There is also a strong link with Keynes's view that deduction is necessary for induction and his preference for using the traditional method of reasoning in economics. Traditional method of reasoning in economics is definitely deductive. Like most economists, he was willing to assume certain direct knowledge, though inconclusive, of the economic phenomena. As he states, instead of demanding demonstrative certainty to begin with, it is preferable to assume small direct knowledge of which further investigation could be advanced.

There is a strong resemblance between Keynes's theory of induction and Russell's theory of induction. Actually, Russell accepts Keynes's theorem on probability. A.J. Ayer (1972, p. 98) states the relationship between theories of Russell and Keynes.

The problem chiefly concerns him, with regard to judgements of degree of credibility, is how to secure a high probability, in this sense, for statements of law. He relies on a theorem of Keynes's according to which a sufficiently long run of exclusively favorable instances bestows on a generalization a probability tending to certainty as a limit provided that the generalization has some initial probability, antecedently to the observation of any of its instances, and provided that if the generalization is false, the probability that we should come across only favorable instances of it tends to zero as the number of those instances increases.

After a close scrutiny, it can be discerned from the above propositions that their import essentially resembles the law of large numbers. That poses a problem that both Russell and Keynes would be intellectually uncomfortable with. The law of large numbers is closely identified with the mathematical probability where as both Keynes and Russell adhere to the notion of degree of credibility. Both believe that some generalizations in minimum should have an initial degree of credibility. If this degree of credibility is to be obtained from the other inductive generalizations on the basis of their resemblance, the argument becomes circular.

Russell constructs an elaborate system of principles for the justification of inductive reasoning. Russell's five principles are (1) postulate of quasi-permanence, (2) postulate of separable causal lines, (3) the postulate of spatio-temporal continuity in causal lines, (4) the structural postulate, and (5) the postulate of analogy. Since the subject at hand here is justification of inductive reasoning and there is a remarkable similarity between Keynes and Russell on this subject, it is worth our while to discuss briefly Russell's five postulates.

The postulate of quasi-permanence assures the existence of material continuants. The postulate of separable causal lines assures that what can be attributed to one and two members in a series will also hold true for other members. The postulate of spatio-temporal assures that in a series of events which are taken to constitute separable causal lines have continuous causality within these series. Its intent is to eliminate action at a distance. The postulate of structure assures that when a number of structurally complex events are separably concentrated at a center, it is usually the case that all belong to causal lines having their origin in an event of the same structure at the center. Finally, the postulate of analogy is to assure that an investigator has reasonable knowledge of the working of minds of others.

A critical examination of Russell's postulate raises some questions. He does not think it is incumbent upon him to prove his postulates because he does not claim them to be analytically true. In his view, to establish them inductively would be circular because inductive reasoning presupposes them. It goes back to the original position of Keynes and Russell that for inductive reasoning some knowledge of the deduction in terms of the major proposition is required. It just goes to show how intractable the problem of induction has been to the best of minds. A.J. Ayer states his disapproval by saying that whatever other purposes they may serve, he does not think they could be used to derive valid inductive generalizations that Russell and Keynes wish to make. Besides they are too general in solving the riddle of induction. Braithwaite (1968, p. 259) does not think the Keynes and Russell approach resolves the riddle of induction.

> But such a supreme major premise, whether in Mill's form of a principle of Uniformity of Nature or in Keynes's form of a principle of Limited Independent Variety, will have to be a logically contingent proposition in order to fulfil the function which is required of it. That it is reasonable to believe such a proposition can then only be justified by an inductive inference. The overwhelming objection to the assimilation of all induction to deduction is that this would require that we should reasonably believe a very general empirical premise, the reasonableness of belief in which would have to be justified by another inductive argument.

Upon reading Keynes's argument on statistical inference and induction, one realizes the intricacy and subtlety that the frequency theory covers up simply by assigning a number to an event. A true inductive generalization, as far as it goes, cannot be modified in the light of an additional and more detailed knowledge about the particular instance. But this cannot be true in the case of statistical induction because the acquisition of further knowledge might make the statistical induction inapplicable but not necessarily less probable in the case of that particular instance according to Keynes. This is so because statistical induction does not pertain to a particular instance as such, but it generalizes about a series of which a particular instance is a random number. Availability of additional information about the particular instance takes away the randomness of that instance and statistical induction is no more applicable to it. Keynes (1973, p. 450) clearly puts this point.

If the acquisition of new knowledge, affords us additional relevant information about the particular instance, so that it ceases to be a random number of the series, then statistical induction ceases to be applicable, but the statistical induction does not for that reason become any less probable than it was—it is simply no longer indicated by our data as being statistical generalization appropriate to the instance under inquiry. The point is illustrated by the familiar example that probability of an unknown individual posting a letter unaddressed can be based on statistics of the Post Office, but my expectation that I shall act thus cannot be so determined.

Towards the end of his book on probability, Keynes, as a good author should, cautions the reader that in order to drive the point home, he has had to display more conviction than he has felt about the subject. Like an advocate, he has had to defend the arguments he put forward.

To cap the discussion on Keynes's theory of probability, it is interesting that it took economists almost half a century after the publication of the *General Theory* to recognize the fact that his theory of probability in every justifiable way is a link in the chain. The topics and subtopics Keynes discerned on in his theory of probability are organically connected with his past probability creation. His views on induction, epistemology and his distrust of quantitative economics seemed to have lasted throughout. But it also remains a fact that economists have failed to recognize and establish that connection. Economists as astute and thorough as Schumpeter also failed to see the full import of the arguments in Keynes's theory of probability. Schumpeter implies that since economics was not enough of an intellectual challenge, Keynes took up the subject bristling with logical niceties yet not entirely without utilitarian connotations?

102

There is no denying the fact that Keynes's main source of inspiration for working on the theory of probability was *Principia Mathematica* by Russell and Whitehead. Furthermore, the influence of G.E. Moore was significant. According to Harrod, it is because of Moore's influence, Keynes thought that probability should be regarded as an indefinable concept. Earlier writers on Keynes such as Dillard, Klein and Hanson have been oblivious of the connection between Keynes's theory of probability and his views on uncertainty, investment and econometrics. Dillard has devoted a chapter to the development of Keynes's thought, which as it is an excellent piece of scholarship, but there is no mention or recognition of Keynes's thoughts on undefinability of probability and induction. Works by the three eminent economists mentioned above are of exceptionally high quality but none of them has recognized the import of Keynes's views on probability and their relevance to his economics. The question sometimes asked, particularly by econometricians, is that after having a written an original and high quality dissertation on a technical subject of probability why did he not continue in that area or at least bestow his blessings on the budding discipline of econometrics?

At this point, one can only surmise on firm and reasonable grounds. As a backdrop it must not be forgotten that at the time Keynes was a King's and a Cambridge man, the universe of mathematics had luminaries of the caliber of G.H. Hardy, Bertrand Russell and Alfred North Whitehead whose names are imprinted in annals of mathematics the civilized world will remember for a long time to come. The situation in statistics was no less glorious for England at that time once one is mindful of the contributors like Karl Pearson, Ronald Fisher, Udney Yule and Jefferys. Keynes, as record shows, was more than tolerably good in mathematics. But he had not had a particular genius in mathematics nor must he had passionate liking for the subject. The question tion that arises then is why has he chosen probability for his dissertation. The answer to this question is that he chose probability, he states this early on in his *Treatise on Probability*, because he was not interested in the mathematics of probability but in the logic of it. To put in a sharper way, he has decided to oppose the school of statistics that wanted to do statistic mathematically. In his essay on Frank Ramsey, Keynes has stated very clearly that in his view probability is concerned with objective relations between propositions as opposed to Ramsey's view that probability should be construed as degrees of belief that could be expressed in terms of calculus. Since Ramsey's degrees of belief could be expressed in probability calculus, it should be regarded as a branch of formal logic. Keynes is willing to give Ramsey ground as far as degrees of belief approach goes, but according to him the degrees of belief approach is not helpful in delineating the area of rational degree of belief from belief in general. Most of all, Keynes (1972, p. 339) thinks that it is not useful in giving a handle on the problem of induction. On the basis of Ramsey's approach, induction becomes merely a useful mental habit—a part of formal logic. Because Keynes thought of induction as objective relations between propositions, the probability calculus is not acceptable to him. This shows that pure mathematics or econometrics were not his preferred area of study. He would rather wrestle with the problem of induction, which by its very nature cannot get away from practicality of life. He distinguishes between formal logic and human logic. Human logic in his view is concerned with the process of induction. This strand and explicit preference for human logic is, in this author's view, a pointer to Keynes exclusive interest and concern for policy matters. As an editor of the *Economic Journal* he went to extraordinary lengths to encourage others to engage in abstract and mathematical theorizing. His encouragement to Frank Ramsey is an example of this.

In his *Causality in Economics* Professor Hicks states three reasons why economists ought to look at causality anew. Like Keynes he also believes that economic facts known to us are very imperfect. Commonly used macro magnitudes such as Gross National Product, Fixed Capital Investment, Aggregate Consumption, Employment and Balance of Payments are imprecise and subject to measurement errors by larger degree than their counterparts in natural sciences. Errors in natural sciences are regarded as tolerable. Since most of the knowledge in economics is uncertain, Hicks suggests that we should start with the study of near-certain knowledge and reduce the degree of uncertainty. It gets progressively harder according to Hicks as one traverses from the penumbra of uncertainty to its core.

The second reason for studying causality in economics according to Hicks is the element of time involved. Cause and effect occur in Hume's view in time. Economists are concerned with the present as historians are concerned with the past. Unlike the task of natural scientists, economists and historians are inevitably involved in dealing with time. Natural scientists are not concerned with historical time because the same experiment could be repeated regardless of date.

The present is moving so fast that a person hardly has time to think of it before it is gone. The image of the present has slid into the past, consequently, economists also have to think of the past. Events taking place today have entirely or partially consequences suspended in the future, so future also becomes a vital concern. Causality is like an octopus that has a foot or two in the past, present and future.

In his explanation of the third reason of the significance of causality in economics, Hicks offers a seemingly simple yet historically important difference in causality, namely, old and new causality. After the occurrence of an event, typically three questions arise, what exactly happened? How it happened? and why it happened? The answer to the third question deals with causality. According to Hicks, the old causality mainly dealt with what happened in occurrence of an event was ascribed to a person or to an 'Act of God'. Hicks (1979, p. 6) puts it clearly.

> One yet can distinguish a system of thought (we might call it old causality) in which causes are always thought as action by someone; there is always an agent, either a human agent or a supernatural agent.

The new causality answers the question why the Newtonian mechanics answered that question for the philosopher-scientists. It was Hume, a philosopher-historian understood it well that human knowledge of the laws was incomplete, but it was capable of being improved. It is the new causality that is fixed in the Adam Smith's title of the *Wealth of Nations*.

As far as economics as a subject and its quantification is concerned, a view expressed by Nicholas Georgescu—Rogen is similar in some respects to that of Keynes. At the outset, Georgescu warns economists that a total ban on using mathematics is contrary to the principle of maximum efficiency—a principle so important in economics—in acquiring knowledge in economics. But he is opposed to the excessive use of mathematics when a simple diagram would serve the purpose with the equal effectiveness. Imitating the quantitative methods of physical sciences, physics in particular, in economics and other social sciences is like not understanding the difference between a blueprint and a simile according to Georgescu. He (1971, pp. 332-33) expressed the point below.

> And the immense satisfaction which understanding derives from arithmomorphic models should not mislead us into believing that their other roles are the same in both social and natural sciences. In physics a model is also "a calculating device, from which we may compute the answer to any question regarding the physical behavior of the corresponding physical system... An economic model being only a simile, can be a guide only for the initiated who has acquired an analytical insight through some laborious training. Economic excellence cannot dispense with "delicacy and sensitivity of touch"—call it art if you wish. And it is only too bad if at times the economist lets himself to be surpassed in this re-

spect by the layman. The widespread view that the economists role is to analyze alternative polices, whereas their adoption is the art of statesmanship, is no excuse. An artless analysis cannot subserve an art.

Georgescu's delicacy and sensitivity can be likened to Keynes's idea of taking the surrounding facts into consideration. Both in economics and probability theory Keynes has held the view, as discussed above, that ready made answers are not possible in economics. This is most likely what Keynes had in mind when he stated that economists need more than a formal command of mathematical economics. He needs the amalgam of logic, intuition and the wide knowledge o facts most of which are not precise. What Georgescu advocates is the tightly reasoned dialectical reasoning for economics. Dialetical reasoning cannot be exact but it can be correct. Schumpeter, in essence, is expounding the same position in the introductory part of *Business Cycles*. Schumpeter states that it is unreasonable to believe that statistical facts alone can be brought to bear the burden of entire analysis. He believes that we must put our trust in bold and unsafe mental experiments or else give up all hope.

This significant confluence of the views of important economists such as Hicks, Keynes, Schumpeter and Georgescu on this important topic under discussion should not be overlooked and underestimated.

9 Viability of Keynesian economics

Like the other epoch-making books in the field of knowledge, Keynes's *General Theory* has aroused a strong reaction and a staunch following. Without any doubt it has served as a fountainhead for different theories and schools of thought. Unlike the classical and neoclassical theories, Keynes has brought out in a sharper focus the misallocation of resources or wastes of resources that occurs in macroeconomic sense. In the late seventeenth century classical economics grew as a mixture of micro elements and macro elements. It was thought to be an intellectual challenge to produce a general theory of the economy as Newton did it in physical science. Such a general system of the economy was predicated on the basis of an individual's instinctive desire for furthering his self-interest and the harmonious self-adjusting system that sets the parameters.

Adam Smith in his *Wealth of Nations* worked out the idea of self-adjusting harmonious system microeconomically in terms of valuation, allocation of resources, distribution, exchange as well as the working of the entire economy in aggregate sense and the dynamics of growth. According to Smith, under the competitive conditions macroeconomic equilibrium, is attained through the equilibrium of saving and investment with flexible wages. Competitive labor and capital markets determine wages and employment, and interest respectively. Automaticity is the unique feature of such a mechanism. The serious lacuna in the classical system was that the monetary sector was never integrated into the system. Both Keynes and Schumpeter were fully aware of this lacuna and tried to enmesh money into their system. This aspect of their system is dealt with at other places in this work. The classicists did not think that the problems of cyclical fluctuations, instability and unemployment were overwhelmingly serious. Malthus showed a serious degree of sensitivity to the problems of periodic fluctuations and the entailing incidence of economic misery on the poor. John Stuart Mill, the last and most influential classical economist of his time, did not realize the seriousness of the problem of cyclical instability and regarded the problem of prolonged and serious unemployment to be contradictory with the free market system.

The classical paradigm was successfully replaced by the theories of the marginal school by 1870. The challenge to the classical school posed by the German historical school did not amount to much. The marginal school developed sharper conceptual tools and was exclusively microeconomic in its orientation. Neoclassical theory was a well chiseled and tightly woven system forged to solve the problems of value, allocation, distribution, exchange and choice. The underlying premises of self-interest and self-adjusting system were kept below the surface. Microeconomics over the time has acquired a sold core which is supposed to have a timeless and universal applicability. The two wheels of the engine of analysis of microeconomic theory are (1) the law of (eventually) diminishing marginal physical product, and (2) the law of diminishing marginal utility. To this Marshall's constancy of marginal utility of money needs to be added to complete the micro analysis.

In the neoclassical realm microeconomics did rule, as it still does in some quarters, as the supreme authority. Economists such as Stigler, Becker and their followers believe even today that the economic theory means or should mean microeconomics. Gary Becker (1971, p. viii) emphatically expresses his preference.

> The perhaps presumptuous title of Economic Theory is used instead of a title Micro Theory or Price Theory because of my belief that there is only one kind of economic theory, not separate theories for micro problems, macro problems, nonmarket decisions, and so on. Indeed the most promising development in recent years in the literature on unemployment and other macro problems has been the increasing reliance on utility maximization and the other principles used to study micro problems.

A comment is made on the last sentence of the above quotation at other places in this work.

The formal structure of the microeconomic theory works through perfect competition to obtain the optimum allocation of resources and achievement of the Pareto optimum. One of the required assumptions of perfect completion is perfect knowledge of the market conditions both on the part of numerous small buyers and sellers. It is because of the smallness of either of a buyer or a seller that reactions to their actions concerning price and output can be disregarded by the rest of the other players. An assumption such as this can be undertaken in microeconomics and optimum allocation of resources can be procured, but in macroeconomics where reality cannot be assumed away it becomes a distorting handicap. The same holds true for the monetary theory because the very existence of money implies uncertainty and lack of knowledge. Uncertainty and erroneous expectations create problems in long-term investment decisions and short-run consumption function. It can be generalized that in neoclassical microeconomics everything is known because what is known is deduced from the premises of perfect competition where as in Keynesian macroeconomics short-run consumption function, marginal efficiency of investment and behavior of liquidity preference schedule are based on uncertainty. It is the uncertain behavior of the above three functions plus downward stickiness of wages that compelled Keynes to create macroeconomics.

Historically and even recently the overwhelming preoccupation of the microeconomic theory has been with the optimum allocation of resources under the conditions of full employment.

In contrast to the analytical quest for the optimum allocation resources in microeconomics, Keynes's was and is a signal effort in this century to make unemployment as the central issue of macroeconomic policy. The waste of labor hours due to prolonged and massive unemployment during a period like the Great Depression or involuntary unemployment above frictional level of unemployment and the cost of unutilized capital that exist as unutilized capacity. Relatively minimum or no attention was paid to these costs in the neoclassical theory of microeconomics. Chronic unemployment did exist throughout the period in all industrial countries besides England. No systematic and conceptualized theorizing was done before Keynes of this undeniable problem of unemployment and unutilized capacity that exists under capitalism. Keynes has not only brought this problem to the center of macroeconomics, unlike Marx and other socialists who also recognized the problem, he has considered the disease as treatable within the framework of capitalistic institutions. According to Marshall, Pigou, Allyn Young deviations from the norm of competition were existent and treatable by taxes and subsidies. According to T.W. Hutchison (1980, p. 17) persistent existence of sizable unemployment under capitalism justifies the use of the word 'General' in the title of General Theory.

There is, nevertheless, one sense in which Keynes's claim to generality for his theory, as opposed to the classical theory, seems to have had validity—that is macroeconomic equilibrium with reasonable full employment, allowing for frictions, had not been the general case historically; rather, as Keynes claimed, a kind of fairly chronic unemployment had prevailed over the centuries.... This kind of unemployment seems to have been general through much of the seventeenth and eighteenth centuries, just as excesses of effective demand, inspired by democratic governments, seem to have become the usual case in the last forty years. Economists have often been prone to assume that last decade or two of their own experience constitutes a general norm of world history or that the economies of other countries and other times have worked just the same way as that of their own country and their own time.

The monetarists believe that the real economic activity is inherently stable and monetary factors, particularly unanticipated changes in the money supply, and other governmental interventions create instability. If uncertainty concerning the money supply and governmental intervention can be minimized or eliminated the economy will stay on the even course. For this money supply should be increased each year by five percent and government should let the market forces have freer play domestically and in international sector.

The dominant paradigm before the *General Theory* was Hayek's theory of business cycle. Hayek has believed in the consistency and practical efficacy in the working of the free market system in creating full employment and price stability. Because of his firm belief in infallibility of the market system, Hayek has to seek the reason for cyclical fluctuations in factors such as money and banking that are outside the market system. Now the interesting point, contradictory in a major way, is that without money the market system cannot be as efficient as it is claimed to be by its proponents. On this important and relevant point one only has to read Dennis Robertson's delightful volume on money which effectively and convincingly discusses the advantages of money to consumers and producers in a market system. To treat money, without which the efficiency potential of the market system cannot be realized, as an outside disturbing factor is contradictory. One is reminded of Schumpeter's poignant remark on this matter, according to which money is a very difficult subject to penetrate fully into, but it should be treated as a kernel and not as a shell. By treating money as an outside intruding factor Schumpeter would say that his fellow Austrian is treating it as a shell.

According to Hayek prices serving as effective signals in equilibrating the forces of demand and supply is the basis for the entire theoretical economics. Consequently, cyclical fluctuations cannot be explained by ignorance or erroneous expectations unless the errors are committed in the process of money creation. Let us briefly sketch Hayek's theory of business cycles as it exists in his *Prices and Production*. In Hayek's business cycle theory, the banking system plays a pivotal role by expanding the credit demanded to exploit rising profitable investment opportunity at the existing money rate of interest. Technical innovations and surge in entrepreneurial expectations lead to a rise in the natural rate of interest. Since the market rate of interest is lower than the natural rate of interest, credit expansion occurs and a higher proportion of current income, higher than the current volume of saving, is invested. Bank credit fuels the expansion and prices rise and at this point 'forced saving' propels the upswing by diverting resources from consumption to investment. Willingness of banks in supplying credit determines the length of the upswing.

As long as the central banks have the discretionary power to expand credit, unlike the gold standard, when entrepreneurial expectations are optimistic demand for credit will always be satisfied and cycles will occur according to Hayek. Hayek has put the banking system and the ever accommodating central bank at the center as far as propelling of the economy into a trade cycle. This creates a theoretical and methodological problem for Hayek which he consciously tried to avoid. If the central bank and banking system is to be regarded as agent provocateurs of business cycle, it amounts to admitting the exogenous factor in the explanation of business cycle for which Hayek himself criticized the non-monetary theories. On the other hand, if the neoclassical theory of profit maximization is to be applied to a bank, then, the infallible equilibrating forces should not allow the disequilibrating process of business cycles. It would be in contradiction with the automaticity of the market system both in micro and macro sense which Hayek firmly believes. Anticipating such a problem, Hayek has insulated himself by not adhering to the perfect knowledge assumption of perfect competition.

The classical and neoclassical concept of perfect competition should not be palatable because all buyers and sellers acting with perfect foresight would behave in such a way to effectively undo the competition. According to Hayek, knowledge is basically unevenly distributed and the variation in belief is what causes competition. In his view, products are not identical but substitutes do exist. Imperfect knowledge, availability of substitutes and product differentiation is a familiar area of monopolistic competition which, no matter how big or small, does result in price being greater than marginal cost and excess capacity. This result is neither palatable nor admissible to Hayek. This aspect of monopolistic competition has been explored in detail at other places.

Despite the theoretical implications of his theory, Hayek was totally opposed to government taking any measures to solve the problems of unemployment. Norman Barry (1981, p. 97) correctly expresses Hayek's view as given below.

Hayek resolutely opposed attempts to stimulate consumer demand, provide public works and prop up the price level because he maintained that the market was self-correcting and that changes in relative prices would tend to harmonize saving and investment intentions which had been discoordinated by monetary disturbance... He did distinguish between an ordinary recession and a genuine deflation (a contraction in money supply which leads to such a fall in demand that there is substantial unemployment of all factors) and implied that different policies apply to these different phenomena. But even in deep depressions Hayek believed that any corrective measures by government were essentially the actions of a desperado.

The classical and neoclassical theories of macroeconomics and micro-economics have been treated at some length because such a treatment fully supplies the background Keynes was up against. It was thought that theoretically a serious and a prolonged depression such as the Great Depression in a free market system was impossible. It has also been emphasized that it was recognized that the use of money does contribute to the welfare of consumer and producer but the role of money was not integrated in macroeconomic sense despite the fact that it was always regarded as the culprit in causing business cycles. Furthermore, the neoclassical economics with its exclusive preoccupation with the microeconomic efficiency became totally oblivious of the waste of resources from macroeconomic unemployment and idle capacity. In this respect, Hla Myint (1948, p. 117) correctly gives a caveat.

In judging the usefulness of the Paretian theory of the Optimum we should avoid two extreme attitudes. We shall not follow the stick-in-the-mud "practical men" and dismiss the whole thing as theoretical toy based on ideal conditions which can never be fully realized in practice. On the other hand, we should not be seduced by its formal elegance and symmetry and get ourselves lost among its theoretical refinements and ideal marginal adjustments which are not likely to involve significant quantities of economic welfare in real life.

In the last sentence Myint makes a very poignant remark because, as he says, microeconomic inefficiencies may not be substantial but, to this it should be added, macroeconomic wastes can be or has been substantial. How do we know the magnitude of the macroeconomic waste? The Keynesians, to their credit, have developed a conceptual and numerical measurement of it. Like most of the measurements of the social phenomena, this too is subject to limitations. But the limitations are such that they do not totally impair the usefulness from the point of view of theory and policy. The reference is here to the famous Okun's law.

As Samuelson (1976, p. 31) reports that Alvin Hansen and his group has been aware of the difference between the actual and potential GNP. Samuelson's statement indicates that Alvin Hansen used to calculate the potential GNP.

> He was uncannily accurate in his back-of-the-envelope estimates of our potential GNP in the 1945-1970 epoch.

Okun's contribution is that he has explicitly attempted to mesh the quantification of the concept in the context of aggregate demand and supply, and in making it a tool and an indicator of the success of such a policy.

The estimated and conceptual difference between the actual and potential GNP is essentially a short-run phenomena and therefore most of the facts about the economy such as technological knowledge, the capital stock, natural resources and skill and education of the labor forces are given data, parameters, and not variables. Okun's is a very careful study in which a crude and common sense observation, with all it's limitations, is turned into a refined and useful policy tool. It must be remembered here that the purpose of the foregone discussion is to realize that like microeconomic waste and inefficiency there can be and is macroeconomic enormous social cost of idle resources. Keynes and the Keynesians such as Okun, Tobin, Samuelson, Solow and others like them definitely deserve all the credit that can be given for making this a theoretical and policy issue in this century. To substantiate the point, it would be highly appropriate to give some of Okun's (1983, pp. 148-58) quantitative estimations below.

> At any point in time, taking previous quarters as given, one percent point more in unemployment rate means 3.3 percent less GNP... Fitted to varying sample periods, the estimated elasticity coefficient ran .35 to .40, suggesting that each one percentage point reduction in employment means slightly less than a 3 percent increment in output (near the potential level)

One could quarrel with Okun's details concerning the assumption regarding labor force participation rate, numbers of hours worked, average productivity but the broad conclusion regarding macroeconomic waste cannot be denied.

The purpose of this effort is to establish the lasting contribution of Keynes and Keynesians of the variety of Samuelson, Tobin, Solow and others like them. Malthus's theory of glut did not make as strong an impact as Keynes's *General Theory* did as far as the lack of effective demand is concerned. This was partly due to Ricardo's superior analytical ability and partly due to the time period. Compared to Malthus, Keynes was a master of polemics and dialectic. On this we have a testimony of a man of an intellectual caliber of Bertrand Russell, which is given at other place in this work. Besides, Keynes had the Great Depression to help him. By the time Keynes's *Great Theory* was conceived and published, the depression was exacerbated to the worst possible degree and this sunk so well in the psyche of the public at large that its existence and severity could not be denied or wished away.

The purpose of the forthcoming analysis is to critically examine the application and performance of the Keynesian economics. There has been pronouncements concerning the dismal failure and alleged death of Keynes (his economics) and Keynesian economics. As pointed out earlier the term Keynesian economics refers in this work to the contributions of right-wing Keynesians such as Samuelson, Solow, Tobin, Lawrence Klein and economists like them. The left-wing Keynesians are Joan Robinson, Sraffa, Kaldor and other economists like them. According to Samuelson (1976, p. 26) more so than Britain, the U.S. was the more appropriate economy for the application of Keynesian economics because it was largely a closed continental economy with an undervalued dollar in which there was an ample scope for increasing autonomous expenditure to attain full employment. Besides, in the monetary sector, despite the large inflows of gold did not lead to the consequent and proportional increase in credit expansion due to the interest in elastic demand for money at relatively lower interest, as predicated by Keynes. Samuelson sketches the correct picture of the situation below.

> I ought to add here that one reason to explain Hansen's importance in carrying the post-1936 ball is that America rather than Britain, was the natural place where the Keynesian model applied: the United States was largely a closed, continental economy with an undervalued dollar that gave ample scope for autonomous macroeconomic policies; Hansen's first Harvard years of the late 1930's, when gold was flowing into this country and, as Hansen said at the time, was providing a massive controlled experiment to show a weak elasticity response to normal easing of credit, that was the era per excellence when an approximation to Keynes's liquidity trap prevailed.

114

As far as the question of liquidity trap is concerned, J.R. Hicks has recently brought in the subject in a historical context. The question has to be dealt with here because, first, it is raised by an eminent economist such as Sir John Hicks and second, it touches a very fundamental question of monetary versus fiscal policy. According to Hicks, the roots of the idea of liquidity trap go all the way to a debate between Keynes and Hawtrey before the days of the *General Theory*. Hicks has stated that both Keynes and Hawtrey believed that the capitalistic system is subject to instability and should be stabilized by using some policy instrument such as monetary policy. Consequently, both were in agreement that the instrument of stabilization should be rate of interest. But the difference arose on short rate versus long rate. Hawtrey preferred a short rate; Keynes preferred a long rate.

In Hick's view, Keynes preferred a long rate because due to a change in the industrial structure fixed capital investment became more important than before. But, Hicks continues by stating that Keynes has found that his long rate was less responsible to changes in the banking policy than Hawtrey's short rate. As a result of the knowledge about this inelasticity of a long rate, Keynes, being interested in speedy results, moved away from monetary policy and opted for fiscal policy. This according to Hicks is the reason for the fiscalism of the *General Theory*. Hicks (1983, p. 15) neatly encapsulates his argument below.

> But then Keynes discovered that his long rate was not only less directly susceptible to banking control than Hawtrey's short, but that it was very likely to be found that just when it was wanted it could move enough. So he moved away from monetary methods to the 'fiscal' methods which have later been so largely associated with his name. That is a process that is taking place inside the *General Theory*... Thus it was, what began as monetary theory became 'fiscalism'.

Hicks's argument as it stands is insufficient to carry the full weight of the argument as to why Keynes had opted entirely for fiscal policy. Purely in the context of the *General Theory*, besides the long term interest inelasticity that Hicks is talking of, there are the consumption and liquidity preference functions that serve as the pillars of the Keynesian structure. The totality of the situation during a severe slump might be such, as Keynes expresses in the *General Theory* (p. 316), that the collapse in the marginal efficiency of capital may be so complete that no practical reduction in the rate of interest will be enough. No simple or single argument such as the one forwarded by Hicks is sufficient to explain or replace the total structure of the *General Theory*. The *General*

Theory may not be a perfectly written book, but it has a logic, very powerful, and a structure of its own. In summary, Keynes's fiscalism cannot be explained by a slow and inadequate response to a long term rate of interest alone.

Despite of Hicks, fiscalism has been an important part of Keynes and Keynesianism, particularly in policy matters. Speaking particularly of fiscal policy, Herbert Stein (1969, p. 282), an economic adviser to the Republican administration has the following to say.

> In fact, the Eisenhower administration did confirm the victory of the fiscal revolution. It accepted without any question the idea of governmental responsibility for the overall performance of the economy and the use of fiscal policy as a primary means of discharging that responsibility.

This indicates that fiscal policy has become an accepted tool of stabilization and growth for the Republicans as it was for the Democrats. But the similarity ends there because the acceptance by the Republicans has been with a grudge and there has been a sustained effort to discredit and overturn the Keynesian doctrine.

As Herbert Stein notes, there was a big drive for a surplus in the budget by Eisenhower in 1959-60. Arthur Burns diagnosed the problem of recession correctly and warned Vice-President Nixon accordingly, but Nixon was not successful in persuading Eisenhower to follow an expansionary policy. The last three Eisenhower years of fiscal policy are recognized as a great mistake. As a consequence of the above policy, there was a recession in 1961 entailing six percent unemployment. Tax receipts were falling and the prospects for the big budget surplus were going to be wiped out. Interestingly enough it was a repetition of the budgetary situation of 1957-58 accompanied by the recession of 1957-58. The mistaken fiscal policy of 1958-60 is what Herbert Stein (1969, p. 370) has called Eisenhower's gift to Kennedy.

> The Eisenhower fiscal policy not only made a contribution, possibly decisive, to the election of a democratic successor, it also made a contribution to the economic program that Democratic administration would follow when in office.

What Setin has said is well agreed upon. But we must not be oblivious of two factors. One, the economy was ready for the Keynesian expansionary fiscal policy. Two, the Kennedy administration cannot merely be regarded as lucky because as it is said by Louis Pasteur 'luck always favors the prepared'.

The evidence of grasping the opportunity with the full knowledge of its potential can be seen in Samuelson's "Economic Frontiers" Report to President Elect Kennedy, January 6, 1961. A very relevant point from the point of view of our discussion to be found in Samuelson's proposal is that, instead of talking simply of a recovery from recession, he has advocated combating the sluggishness that plagued the American economy. He has strongly advocated that a strong expansionary policy should be devised to make the economy operate in a zone of full employment and full capacity utilization which would enable the economy to close the gap between the actual and potential GNP. Samuelson (1966, pp. 1479-80) forcefully expresses his argument.

> Had our economy progressed since 1956—not at a dramatic sprint of Western European and Japanese economies or at the rush of the controlled totalitarian systems but simply at the modest pace made possible by our labour force and productivity trends—we could have expected 1961 to bring a Gross National Product some 10 percent above the 1500 billion level we are now experiencing. With unemployment below 4 percent, with overcapacity put to work, and with productivity unleashed by economic opportunity, such a level of activity would mean higher private consumption, higher corporate profits, higher capital formation for the future and higher resources for much needed public programs.

Nobody can blame a person or a government for putting their best foot first. But Samuelson warns against, what he considers as a misleading practice, telling the public that this or that is now at an all time high. This in his view diverts attention away from insistence on realizing full macroeconomic potential. Unfortunately, this practice still continues in the public pronouncements of government officials and some economists.

In the above mentioned report, Samuelson is fully aware of the potential danger of inflation that could have entailed the expansionary fiscal policy. To Samuelson (1966, p. 1482), energizing the slackened economy to capture the potential GNP seemed to have been more important than the potential danger of inflation. According to him, a program that could have tolerated stagnation in the American economy could have prevented the U.S. from making those improvements in industrial productivity that were desperately needed to preserve American competitiveness in the international market. In this trade-off between inflation and economic growth, his choice was clearly for growth. President Kennedy being an intellectual himself was receptive to new ideas in economics. He himself was capable of abstract thinking and sought, far more vigorously than the previous presidents, instruction and advice from economists. He was, because of his openness to fresh ideas, able to assemble a coherent group of brilliant advisers who were instrumental in translating the Keynesian economics into workable policy premises. Herbert Stein (1969, p. 379) who is an economist of opposite persuasion, though of a moderate variety, has stated the following regarding the Kennedy economists.

> The economists in turn had exceptional qualities. They were, for one thing, extremely self-confident. Of course, anyone who becomes an adviser to a President is likely to be self-confident, but there are degrees of this. The Kennedy economists were, in the main, of that generation which had been most moved intellectually and emotionally by Keynes's *General Theory*. They were neither so old as to have learned grudgingly and with qualifications nor so young as to have first met it as an already well-established doctrine... The Keynesian movement swept economics... Now its leaders were coming victoriously to Washington to practice what they had been teaching.

The Keynesianism that arrived in Washington in the early Sixties was nurtured and refined assiduously by Alvin Hansen, Paul Samuelson, James Tobin, Lloyd Metzler, Richard Musgrave, Robert Solow and others of their persuasion. Policy-wise and chronologically important step is the 1964 tax cut. The Johnson administration that succeeded the Kennedy administration emphasized the significance of a balanced budget once the economy attains full employment. The economy did attain full employment in 1965, but ever increasing expenditures for the Vietnam War did not make budget balancing possible. President Johnson in 1967 unsuccessfully tried to get support for a tax increase in order to avoid the budget deficit. In addition, the Great Society program expenditures were added. According to Herbert Stein, many people, particularly businessmen and some conservative economists did not object as much to the use of fiscal policy as they did to the idea of secular stagnation and consequent expenditures, the emphasis on redistributive taxation, denial of the role of incentives in investment decisions and rejection of the role of monetary policy.

The large tax reduction that President Kennedy requested in 1963 was enacted into a law during the early part of the Johnson administration. As it is well known that President Johnson had the experience, connections in the Congress and negotiating skills to turn the proposal into a law. As a result of this bill individual income taxes were reduced by about $8 billion in 1964 and $11.5 billion in 1965. The accompanying corporate tax reduction in 1964 and 1965 approximately by $1.8

billion and $3 billion respectively. The outcome was an increase in GNP by $25 billion in 1964 and $30 billion in 1965. The figures should be interpreted as estimates. Such outcomes provided important analytical substantiation that Revenue Act 1964 fulfilled the expectations of its proponents, and that it supplied a powerful stimulus to economic expansion.

Above results were acceptable to most economists. With such success, the Keynesians thought that economy could be managed with some degree of precision towards full employment. Walter Heller (1968, pp. 7-8) expressed this confidence in the management of the American economy.

> By implication it also shows that our quantitative understanding of the economy's operation has reached the point where policy can aim for full-employment target with some precision. In planning the tax cut, the employment target was translated into a required increment to total output and demand. The policy changes needed to bring forth this much demand were estimated from what was known of the behavior of consumer and businesses. And the results were very much what economists had expected they would be. The successes of the recent years have made clear to the public what has been clear to the economist for some time. We can keep the economy at or near its potential and reduce frequency and severity of economic downturns far better than we have been.

The issue under discussion here now is after such an impressive success what did go wrong that has substantially deviated the economy from the path to the promised land? Factually things did go wrong substantially. The next question is how much can Keynes and Keynesians be blamed for that. If both of them cannot be blamed, who or what else is responsible for the failure? In this context it is appropriate to discuss how dead is Keynes?

James Tobin has reduced the gist of General Theory into four propositions and tried to test their survivability in terms of issues and policies over time. Not all economists are likely to agree with Tobin concerning the central spirit and content of General Theory. Nevertheless Tobin's propositions serve as a starting point for our discussion.

First, according to Tobin, in matured capitalist economies, the response of wages and prices is slow to the forces of excess demand and supply, especially more so to excess supply. The delayed and anemic response of wages and prices does not allow the economy to vigorously attain full-employment equilibrium without inflation. Matured capitalistic economies tend to crawl by fits and starts towards equilibrium never quite attaining it.

Second, as a sequel to the above process, persistent involuntary unemployment takes a heavy toll in terms of foregone labor hours and output. The unemployed willing to work at or below the existing real wage cannot find jobs and are not successful in signaling their availability.

An interesting point could be interjected here. Economists like Harry Johnson have expressed the view that the Great Depression was an aberrant interlude in the history of capitalism. Frankel and Johnson (1976, p. 25) express this view as given below.

> More fundamentally, the assumption of normally full employment reflects the passage of time and accumulation of experience of reasonably full employment as the historical norm rather than the historical rarity that Keynes's theory and left-wing mythology made it out to be.

A careful discernment is in order here. Depressions, severe recessions and resulting unemployment is more a matter fact than of ideology as Johnson and Frankel make it out to be. Factually it can be shown that lasting and serious episodes of unemployment have not been as uncommon as Chicago people like to think. How the left-wing Keynesians and right-wing Keynesian and Chicago economists explain it is not the issue at hand here, but simply its existence.

T.W. Hutchison, whose work has been referred to before and who is not a left-wingish Keynesian, has stated that British economists such as Foxwell, Malthus and a politician, Joseph Chamberlain, were concerned about the recurrent and periodically lasting unemployment. A caveat must be added to our discussion because compilation of records on unemployment from historical perspective are recent. Besides, of the available records it would be extremely difficult to decompose various kinds of unemployments such as seasonal technological and involuntary. With these qualifiers in mind, it still would be a viable proposition, on the basis of the evidence presented by Foxwell, that there must have episodes of substantial magnitude of time and number present historically as far as unemployment is concerned.

Third, long run capital formation is determined by entrepreneurial profit expectations and attitude towards uncertainty according to Keynes. Most economists are likely to accept this proposition but reading between lines would indicate that he has a twist in mind. According to him in a profit oriented and profit-driven economy marginal efficiency, which determines investment, will be high if there is enough aggregate demand. Therefore maintaining aggregate demand is necessary for capital formation, growth, survival and thriving of capitalism.

Four, in a monetary economy, in opposition to the flex price and wage real economy of the classicists, flex price and wage would not create the conditions of full employment through the working of the free market forces.

The basic question to be answered is what did go wrong with the economics of Keynes and Keynesian economics? The tax cuts of the 1960s definitely set the economy on its way to expansion. Then came the Great Society program and the Vietnam War. U.S. fought a major war and initiated the Great Society program at a point when the economy was at full employment and there was no deficiency of aggregate demand. Either taxes should been raised or some expenditures should have been reduced but neither was done. President Johnson's economic advisers suggested a tax increase. Circumstances were such that neither the Congress nor the public would have approved the tax increase for that war. One way out, temporarily an easy way out, was to finance the war by deficit spending. It was an expensive and protracted war. James Buchanan (1970, p. 173) has provided a magnitude of the expenditures for that period.

> In absolute terms, outlays on national defense are impressive. For fiscal year 1970, more than $81 billion was initially budgeted for this item. This was only slightly below one eleventh of the predicted value for gross national product. Hence, for purposes of simple approximation, we may consider that $1's worth of each $11 produced in the United States is related directly to national defense outlay. And for comparative purposes, it is again interesting to note that this share in GNP remained roughly stable over the 1965-70 period.

The above magnitude indicates that military spending added substantially to the aggregate demand at a time when the economy was at or near full employment. This is not in agreement with Keynes. Inflation took deep roots at this time which have not yet been fully eradicated. Tobin, (1978, p. 437) who has had a personal involvement as a member of the Council of Economic Advisors for Kennedy-Johnson administrations, captures the spirit and frustration of that decade.

> The 1960s began with high promise for American life, but much of it was lost in Vietnam. The economic dimension is perhaps the least important, but serious enough. The War on Poverty petered out, the dream of Great Society was not fulfilled, the grand macroeconomic design was discredited. The economy resumed an unstable course, with stubborn inflation and, in the 1970's, excessive unemployment too. Lyndon Johnson bravely fought to combine guns and

butter, to prevent his great society programmes from being sacrificed for military spending... But in 1966 the economy could not finance both without an increase in taxes. Deficit financing overheated the economy and began the era of inflation and instability still afflicting us.

The calamitous war, impossibility of raising taxes and the consequent deficits are hardly Keynes's fault. On the contrary, the focus of Okun's law in terms of the loss of out to the economy in macroeconomic sense due to unemployment and unutilized capacity represents a theoretical and empirical advance in theory and policy. Okun's law shows a quantitative relationship between the GNP gap and unemployment gap. This relationship has become an important macroeconomic analytical tool and is shown to be sufficiently stable and reliable over the past two decades to be called a law. Robert Gordon's (1984, p. 561) in-depth and careful study concerning Okun's law has shown the following results.

It appears that natural or potential real GNP,Q, which measures how much the economy can produce when operating at its natural rate of unemployment, roughly 6.0 since 1975, grew by 3.75 percent per year between 1960 and 1974, 3.35 percent per year between 1974 and 1979, and 2.80 percent per year since 1979.

The slowdown in potential GNP per year since 1979 is explained by Gordon. The major concern here is to show that the loss has been real and substantial. In this context, it is of prime importance to realize the real thrust of Keynes's argument. Keynes has not been merely concerned about pulling the economy out of the doldrums of the Great Depression. The main thrust of his argument has been not to let the economy slide into a recession or a depression. Of course, this amounts to saying the same thing that actual GNP should approximate the potential GNP as closely as possible.

At this point, what is needed is a pointed and clear response to the question of the death (end) of Keynesian economics. Samuelson's remark below indicates the width and depth to which Keynesian influence has been permeated in the writing those who want to refute Keynes. According to Samuelson (1986, p. 262) when Milton Friedman expressed his analytics of monetarism it came out to be nothing but one specialization of the general Keynesian identities and behavior functions that are not plausible. Similarly, Benjamin Friedman has proven that the preferred theory of Karl Brunner and Allen Meltzer, in equation form, was never seen in pre-1933 literature and have to be qualitatively identical to the Keynesian models of James Tobin.

An important point, as a sort of finale, is that 'the cat is out of the bag.' Friedman has always claimed that there has been a subtle oral tradition of the quantity theory of money at the University of Chicago identical to the modern quantity theory of money expounded by Friedman. This point was first openly discussed by Patinkin, a Chicago graduate, stating that this so called subtle oral tradition was never there. The monetary theory at Chicago was the same monetary theory of Robertson and Marshall as it was taught everywhere according to Samuelson. The import of the argument here is that the new incarnation of the quantity theory propounded by Friedman has been influenced by the monetary analysis of Keynes's *General Theory*. Friedman has every right to construct a theory he wants to. Fighting fire with fire is also a legitimate tactic. The question here is, for legitimacy and respectability, claiming something that was not there. Samuelson's point is that had this tradition been there before the publication of *General Theory*, Chicago monetary theorists such as Lloyd Mints and Jacob Viner should have used it. But it was not. In a way, Friedman is attributing a view to economists who did not hold such a view. Most importantly, Friedman's quantity theory is influenced by Keynes.

Of Tobin's four propositions concerning Keynes's economics, the first three, on the basis of facts most economists would agree, are consistent with the working of matured capitalistic countries. The flex price and wage world of classical capitalism does not exist. Persistence of large unemployment is not uncommon. Entrepreneurial decisions concerning long form capital investment depend on expectations regarding profit and risk.

Robert Barro's (1979, pp. 54-63) analysis of Keynesian economics attributes the failure of economic policies, allegedly based on Keynesian economics, to what he calls the deeper economic elements such as imperfect information about the present or future, factor mobility cost, or transaction costs. These are mostly market imperfections. James Tobin's (1982, p. 91) reply is as brief as it is pungent.

It takes a heap of Harberger Triangles to fill an Okun Gap.

Barro's is a clearly written analysis of the events and policies but, interestingly enough, there is no mention of Vietnam War expenditures and lack of political economic consensus it created. As noted earlier, the war has proven to be a nemesis of the promise of the 1960s and of the grand design of economic policy.

Central focus of this discussion is viability of the economics of Keynes against vituperative attacks. In this concern, a fresh strand of defense has been launched by Michael Surrey (1988, pp. 107-124) in his explanation of what he calls as the Great Recession of 1974-84. Surrey calls his defense Keynesist as opposed to the Clower-Leijonhvfrud interpretation which he calls Keynesian. The term he uses for Samuelson-Hicks-Tobin Keynesianism is neoclassical synthesis. According to Surrey, Keynes attacked the neoclassical orthodoxy on four points. First, Keynes rejected the view that in absence of market imperfections capitalist economy will automatically attain full employment equilibrium. Second, Keynes questioned the neoclassical neglect of money in the determination of the rate of interest. Third, Keynes seriously questioned the direction of causation postulated by the neoclassical orthodoxy. Fourth, Keynes considered the supply/demand/price analytics to be systematically and fundamentally unsuited for macroeconomic relationships.

In Surrey's view, the first two points were comfortably incorporated into the neoclassical synthesis. Integration of the real balance effect and derivation of the vertical Phillips curve in macroeconomics has engulfed the Keynesist economics by making it a special case of the neoclassical economics. But this cannot be right according to Surrey, as noted earlier, because Keynes insisted on calling his grand design the *General Theory*. Consequently, the powerful sparks of the Keynesian revolution must be looked for somewhere else in Keynes's economics. Besides, what was it that Keynes was struggling to escape from when he says that he has had a 'long struggle to escape from the orthodox theory'? To assume and then believe that economy believes the way orthodox theory states is to assume away the problem. Why is it that the orthodox theory was unable to answer the question of what would be the effect on unemployment of money wage reduction? Surrey (1988, p. 109) neatly states his position.

> Our argument is that Keynes did in fact show that the supply/demand/price system is systematically wrong as a basis for macroeconomic theory, but that he was partially successful in adumbrating a solution. Nevertheless, an examination of two key elements in the argument of the *General Theory* will give some idea of the real, or latent, Keynesian revolution.

Next, Surrey deals with the question of the direction of causation or the problem of identification in econometric terms. Keynes's criticism of the classical theory centered around the two elements. First, making savings dependent on the rate of interest neglects the effect of changes in income. Second, if income depends on the level of investment, saving and investment schedules logically cannot shift independently. In econometric terms saving schedule is mis-specified (it leaves out an important variable) and the correct identification of the simultaneous r/I/Y/s makes it under-identified. According to Meghnad Desai (1976, pp. 17-18), identifiability of a relation essentially implies that, given the supposed causal foundation of the model, the data are capable of estimating the relation, as opposed to inadvertently estimating another relation of the same form within the same causal structure.

After the correct specification the system could be expressed as given below.

$$I = f(A,r)$$
$$S = f(Y,r)$$
$$I = s$$

A stands for autonomous expenditure or state of expectation. But there is no solution to this system because r and y are two fundamental endogenous variables for which there is only one exogenous variable, A. For a given value of A, level of Y can be derived when r is given. Since the objective was to determine r, this exercise is unproductive.

But Keynes's objection is much more fundamental than this. The system, besides being indeterminate, is also under-identified in terms of s/r and I/r. According to Surrey, in graphical terms, this implies that no meaning whatsoever can be attached to points on either the savings schedule or on the investment schedule except the single observed point indicating the confluence of S, I and r. This is precisely what Keynes had in mind when talks about the need to be able to hypothesize independent shifts in the two schedules. When the investment schedule shifts due to autonomous changes in expectations, saving remaining fixed, the points of intersection of two schedules depict or identify the saving schedule. On the contrary, when saving schedule shifts without any change in the investment schedule, the resulting intersection depicts or identify the investment schedule. Significance of the identification problem in empirical estimation cannot be denied. But it is equally important in theory because if the points defining a schedule cannot in principle be determined its theoretical foundation becomes awfully shaky.

Keynes's system, given below, is determined and fully identified.

$$I = f(A,r)$$
$$s = f(Y,r)$$
$$Md = f(Y,r)$$
$$Ms = M$$
$$I = s$$
$$Md = Ms$$

In this system, the two fundamentally endogenous variables are Y and r and two exogenous variables are A and M. Investment, saving and demand-for-money functions are each exactly identified. Supply of money is the new exogenous variable brought in the system. Surrey (1988, p. 113) believes that this is the fundamental revolution that Keynes intended bring in economic theory.

> It is our contention that the really fundamental character of the revolution intended to be wrought by the *General Theory* lay in the rejection by Keynes of the prior and still more fundamental second step. Put it briefly, if supply and demand schedules cannot be separately identifiable (in the technical sense), the notion of a gap between them is vacuous and the presence and absence of an auctioneer to make market signals 'effective' simply does not arise.

This 'identification' revolution created by Keynes was not sustained by Keynes and by Keynesians of all leanings according to Surrey. In his (Surrey's) view Keynes reverted back to neoclassical orthodoxy in his theory of inflation, expounded in *How to Pay for the War* (1941), and international trade, particularly, in Bretton Woods and Washington Loan negotiations. This was not because Keynes abandoned his own revolution, but because he was overextended in his public commitments and, consequently, had no time to apply his revolutionary analysis to the other branches of economics according to Surrey. Surrey thinks had Keynes been able to spend ten years at Kings instead of at Whitehall, he would have extended his revolution and the world would have been better off.

Surrey has attempted to apply the Keynesist economics to the problems of inflation and international trade. He (1988, p. 116) expressed his agenda in the following words.

> In widening Keynes' analysis to provide a 'Keynesist' account of the problems of an open, inflation-prone managed economy, we need to provide extensions to Keynes' more limited analysis of a closed, fixprice economy. These extensions should satisfy the criteria of identifiability (and consequential question of endogencity, exogencity and causality) and the looser but equally important proposition that the market model generally fails the identifiability test, quantity reactions to changes in exogenous variable will generally be more powerful than price reactions.

Interpreting Keynes and mining the *General Theory* is a sizable industry in economics. With a relatively open entry, this is to be expected.

Nevertheless, it cannot be denied that it also adduces to Keynes's greatness as an economist. Surrey has every right to interpret Keynes as he wants to. But to let the entire burden of Keynesian revolution be borne by identification and causality is very much open to debate. This issue will be critically examined but first it is imperative to study Surrey's expansion and application of the Keynesist theory to inflation and international trade.

As far as inflation is concerned, according to Surrey Keynesist analysis states that the real wage is determined by the demand for labor. If so, a change in the money wage will create a change in the price, given the level of employment. Consequently on the basis of the Keynesist logic, a change in unit wage costs will change the general price level. In an open economy, unit costs are also susceptible to changes in import unit costs, which incorporate in them changes in world prices, exchange rate and indirect taxes. Thus according to the Keynesist theory, inflation has its origin in money wage and other unit costs.

In the case of trade theory Surrey thinks that in a two-country trade model, identification of each country's offer curve requires that shifts in other's offer curve do not alter its own. This is not tenable because import demand is made to be a function of domestic demand and the terms of trade, which amounts to saying that no full employment is assumed. In such a situation foreign trade multiplier will have repercussions in both countries and offer curves of both countries cannot shift independently of each other. From the point of view of the Keynesist theory, this charge puts the trade theory in an unavoidable predicament: (1) by ignoring the dependence of imports on domestic income and relative prices, the import functions are mis-specified, and (2) upon recognizing such dependence, the system becomes under-identified.

According to Surrey, the solution to such a predicament is reconstruction of trade theory which incorporates both income and price influences on trade flows, consumption, production and employment. Absence of such a trade theory in his view shows that the Keynesian revolution in this sense is incomplete.

Importance of causality and the identification problem cannot be denied or overlooked. Franklin Fisher (1966, p. 2) states that in simultaneous equation context it does not suffice to know that equation to be estimated contains precisely a specified list of variables, but it is also necessary to know what variables are contained in other simultaneously holding equations or to have other information about the equation under consideration. In absence of such an information, structural estimation is a near impossibility. No amount of detailed and complete empirical information allows one to identify the equation. For structural estimation, additional prior information must be brought to bear.

On the basis of the above information it must be admitted that once money supply is treated as an endogeneous variable, as it is done in the neoclassical IS-LM system, it becomes under-identified. Keynes's solution to this was an independent account of the determination of the rate of interest by treating money supply as an exogenous variable.

In the production and employment sector, there are three endogenous variables, the level of output, Y, the level of employment, N, and the level of real wage, w/p. There are only two equations for the above three variables. One, a production and employment function relating Y and N. Two, a profit-maximizing condition in which real wage w/p equals the value of the marginal product of labor. The system, thus, becomes under-identified. The neoclassical solution, which Surrey considers demonstrably invalid, is to treat Y to be exogenous. Keynes's solution, which Surrey prefers, is that it lets Y be independently determined by way of consumption function. Consequently, the system becomes identified.

At this point in our discussion, it might be important to be mindful of Klein's (1965, P. 18) caveat on identification.

Identification cannot be cheaply achieved in any particular investigation by simply adding some weak or marginal variable to one of the relationships of a system. One must add something substantial and significant which had been previously neglected.

On the basis of Klein's above consideration it can be argued that Surrey has a point. Aggregate demand, of which consumption forms a major part, is important in determining aggregate supply, Y. Surrey's criticism of the Mill-Marshall offer curve is also methodologically sound, but that itself cannot and does not constitute as an argument against free or freer trade.

It must not be forgotten that the central issue here is the viability of Keynes and his economics. Surrey's work, at the least, can be taken as a vital sign of Keynes's viability. It is also stated above that Samuelson has shown that the monetarists have incorporated Keynesian elements in their system. T.W. Hutchison, not a Keynesian, as noted above, has shown that in England there have been many episodes of chronic and substantial unemployment which were not paid attention to by Ricardo and others like him. Malthus, who was aware of this malady, repeatedly drew attention to this problem. In this century it was Keynes who took up the challenge and did what Malthus could not. Analytically he created a theory, a general theory at that, that can incorporate unemployment. This is his everlasting contribution.

10   The age of Schumpeter

Herbert Giersch has stated in May 1984 issue of *American Economic Review* that the fourth quarter of this century should rightly be called the age Schumpeter. John R. Hicks in his *Crisis in Keynesian Economics* has stated that the third quarter of the century in economics belongs to John Maynard Keynes and should be called the age of Keynes. The third quarter of this century is a past and can be objectively and critically examined in terms of Keynes's influence on economic theory and policy. Three-fifths of the last quarter of the century has passed and a certain objective judgment could be arrived at on Schumpeter in terms of his on-going influence on the vital areas of the economic theory and empirical research.

It has been amply discussed in this work that Keynes's influence on macroeconomics has been nothing short of overwhelming. It has also been stated in this work that Schumpeter wanted to succeed Walras in building a dynamic system of the capitalistic economy. Schumpeter thought that Walras was the greatest economist ever because he constructed an elegant general equilibrium system in mathematical terms. This Schumpeter thought to be Walras's achievement par excellence. But the greatest lacuna of the Walrasian system was that it was static. From the point of view of the analytical developmental of economics Schumpeter was generously willing to give credit to Walras for his static mathematical general equilibrium system. But it must be understood that Schumpeter could not have possibly believed that Walras really captured the spirit and soul of capitalism. To him, the essence of capitalism consists in the perpetual gale of creative destruction that is due to the entrepreneur. The placid and aesthetic beauty of perfect competition leading to optimum allocation of resources is just something to start with theoretically. In his view, capitalism is nothing if not dynamic. Personal actions, instead of the impersonal forces of the market, determine the prices of products and resources.

Schumpeter (1989, p. 104) expresses his views on Walras in the following way.

> I for one shall always look up to Leon Walras as the greatest of all economists. In his theory of general equilibrium he gave a powerful basis to all our work. It is true that while he made the decisive step in the quantitative, he failed to move in the numerical line, the junction of which two is characteristics of econometrics.

Schumpeter wanted to create that dynamic economic system. In this sense, he wanted to do what Walras did not and the discipline of economics needed the most. Marx, he knew, had the dynamics with the unessential baggage of Hegelian dialetics. But the content of Marxian dynamics was all wrong. According to Schumpeter, entrepreneurs are no exploiters, on the contrary, they are the ones who made silk stockings available to village girls. In Marx, capitalists exploit workers and big capitalists swallow small capitalists. In the Schumpeterian system, worker's exploitation by capitalists does not exist, and in a recession, when market contracts to eliminate excess capacity consolidation does occur. Schumpeter's dynamics is exclusively his own, though some elements of this dynamics could be found scattered in the writings of earlier economists. J. B. Say did emphasize the role of entrepreneur but did not integrate it in the grand system as Schumpeter has done.

Creation of the most needed dynamics entirely in the form of a grand system which Schumpeter created in *Economic Development* was not recognized and followed, in this author's view, in the way Schumpeter expected. In concern with Keynes and Schumpeter the Great Depression has played an important role. Occurrence, depth and persistence of the depression gave birth to *The General Theory*. Had the depression not occurred, Keynes might still have done something of significance, given his extraordinary ability, but it would have been very unlikely to be of the magnitude of *The General Theory*. As Samuelson has stated Keynes has turned the flow of the river and has proven himself to be a Wagnerian hero. The plain fact is that the opportunity came and Keynes seized it in the most extraordinary way. Maybe, just maybe, Marshall had an inkling or a premonition of this and that was the reason why Marshall went to great lengths to persuade Keynes to stay in economics. Of course, all this is highly conjectural.

The depression exactly had an opposite effect on Schumpeter. Ironically, he was an expert in the area of business cycles and just about at the same time wrote two volumes on business cycles. All the ingredients of his grand design are included in Schumpeter's theory of business cycles. But in midst of the depression it became a formal exercise. As it is noted at other places in this work, according to Peter Drucker, Schumpeter had composed a work quite similar to Keynes's *General Theory* but decided not to complete and publish it because he (Schumpeter) thought Keynes's work superseded his. The purpose of this work is not to pit Schumpeter against Keynes. It is undertaken with the conviction that contributions of both have enduring values as far as the theory and practice of economics is concerned.

Another simple and obvious yet important observation that needs to be made is that in the post-depression era of Keynesianism and developmental planning it was highly unlikely for a Schumpeterian entrepreneur to be a hero. Macroeconomics emphasizing the deficiency of aggregate demand almost took entrepreneur, innovations and aggregate supply for granted. Aggregate supply in such a milieu as the above was never thought to be a serious problem.

The last quarter of this century might very well be called the age of Schumpeter, but even if it is not, in this author's view, it would not and should not make an iota of difference as far as Schumpeter's place and reputation as one of the greatest economists of all time is concerned. But it also cannot and should not be denied that due to the overwhelming preoccupation of the economists with the macroproblems during the post-depression period, certain aspects of Schumpeter's contribution have been overlooked. This is particularly true of his later contributions.

The purpose of the following discussion is to examine these contributions. Schumpeter designed a grand dynamic economic system in his *Theory of Economic Development*. It will be realized from the forthcoming discussion that Schumpeter firmly retained his convictions in all the elements of his grand design despite of his *Capitalism, Socialism and Democracy*. Chronologically, contributions that are proposed to be discussed below are later than Capitalism, Socialism and Democracy. It is clear from the study of these contributions that in some instances he is belaboring the points that he thought were either misunderstood or were not fully understood. In other instances, he added some refinements. We propose to discuss important elements of the Schumpeterian system in the context pointed out above.

One of the important elements in the Schumpeterian system is the role of banks and their credit creation which plays a vital role in the initial stages of economic development. Important implications follow from Schumpeter's theory as far as this aspect is concerned. One, Schumpeter plainly states that in a situation where banks finance entrepreneur's ventures through credit creation, banker's involvement in the operation and management of that enterprise is inevitable and unavoidable. In the quotation below Schumpeter (1949, 1965, p. 59) sharply emphasizes the role of banks and credit creation.

"Credit creation" introduces banks and quasi-banking activities. Here we meet with the difficulty that orthodox banking theory, emphasizing as it does current financing of current trade transactions as the main function of banks had to do with bringing into existence new industries. French and German experience offers a rich field for the study of this phenomenon, and the common saying that in the United States enterprise developed so well because its banking system was so bad also indicates an important truth: after all, we should not simply shut our eyes or sanctimoniously disapprove when we find that in certain cases even railroad building was financed by the issue of bank notes.

As far as the banker's involvement or supervision in business enterprise is concerned, Schumpeter (1949, 1965, p. 59) states it in the following way.

.... it stands to reason that a bank which finances the overhead of a new enterprise must at the very least supervise very closely the behavior of the enterprise founded. That is to say, the necessity of supervising customers which exists to some extent even for the most ordinary routine business acquired in the case envisaged a novel importance.

Schumpeter is careful in pointing out that supervision the banks have done in industrialized countries has definitely varied from time to time and country to country. But in his view this important phenomenon has not been adequately studied by economists. To him, adequate study of the relationship between enterprises and financing banks from the point of view of economic history is necessary to build a sound economic theory. Entrepreneurs were far from happy about the restrictions the bankers imposed and fought against them. Some entrepreneurs, such as John Law and Periere Brothers themselves became bankers to escape the tyranny of bankers according to Schumpeter.

The phenomenon of credit creation by banks during the early stages of economic development has been extremely unpalatable to modern economists. Somehow it creates the impression that economic development could occur with money capital. It should be made clear though that Schumpeter thought of it as one of the important sources of finance. This element of Schumpeter makes the classical, neoclassical and even the Marxists extremely uncomfortable.

In the 1949 publication, Schumpeter discusses various sources of finance for an enterprise in its earlier stages including credit creation by banks. His position seems softer than the one taken in *Business Cycles*. He has considered credit creation as a monetary complement of innovation. He (1939, 1964, p. 85) strongly states his position in the following way.

Those "funds" consists in means of payment created ad hoc. But although in themselves these propositions are nothing but pieces of analytic scaffolding, to be removed when they serve their purpose, the logical relation which they embody, between what is called "credit creation by banks" and innovation will not be lost again. This relation, which is fundamental to the understanding of the capitalist engine, is at the bottom of all problems of money and credit at least far as they are simply problems of public finance.

Schumpeter believed in building a sound theory on the foundations of historical facts. This point will be fully dealt with in the forthcoming discussion. Schumpeter utilized substantial German historical data as a raw material for his theory, particularly the idea of a banker involving himself closely in the supervision of an enterprise. Kindleberger (1978, p. 200) concurs with Schumpeter on this point.

It may be doubted that the banker's decisions were in fact decentralized. Openheim, Hansemann, Mevissen, von der Heydt in Cologne; Bleichroder, Mendelssohn in Berlin, Rothchild in Frankfurt were tied into one another's activities, as well as into industry. Mevissen was an officer or director of six banks, eight industrial corporations and a railroad. He admitted that the government wanted to develop industry, but keep it under tutelage. His intimate friend, Vierson, had eight directorships further.

Richard Tilly's work provides enough corroborative evidence on the nature and extent of credit creation by the banks in Germany. In his discussion, Tilly discusses a prevalent practice of drawing a dry bill. A dry bill is a bill in which a drawer and a drawee were the same person. Tilly (1966, pp. 70-71) discusses the practice of dry bills.

But though it was important to be aware of distinctions like this, such caution does not seem to have been customary. Indeed one of the most striking features of commercial practice in Rhineland at this time was the widespread use of dry bills as a means of payments. In 1845 proponents of joint-stock note-issuing bank pointed out to the large circulation of such bills as one of the greatest evils to be overcome by the government's approval of their plans.... Contemporaries clearly recognized that the bankers—even without the right of issue—could create money through their lending and current account arrangement.

From the above evidence, of which Schumpeter had knowledge and understanding in depth, it is not hard to surmise why he remained skeptical about the theory-building enterprise in economics.

The above should not be construed in the sense that Schumpeter was against theory. On the contrary, he strongly believed in the innate power of the theory as an engine economic analysis. One of the best discernments, if not the best, Schumpeter has done on the subject is contained in his about 25 page review of Mitchell's work on business cycles. It is well known that Mitchell and Burns's exhaustive statistical work on business cycles under the auspices of the National Bureau of Economic Research was done without much solid theoretical foundations and has been subject to an intense debate such as the Koopmans versus Rutledge Vinning debate. Schumpeter's criticism of Mitchell's work is in the same spirit. But a mere suggestion by Mitchell that his work might lead to reformulations of economic theory had delighted Schumpeter (1989, pp. 73-74) to state the following.

One of the best things said in the volume before us, is the suggestion (p. 452), "that ideas developed in the study of business fluctuations may lead to reformulations of economic theory."

Schumpeter has done this lengthy review very carefully and incisively. He clearly states that as important as statistical facts and experiments are, without the analytical tools of theory to interpret statistics, experiments and results is like going backward in scientific research. Schumpeter (1989, p. 75) forcefully puts his views on this point.

True, Professor Mitchell does not take kindly to what savors of "theoretical construction" and his preferences, while toned down both by scrupulous fairness and by his invariable courtesy and generosity, are yet clear enough. He can hardly help associating the work of theorists with insufficient command over fact with ways of thinking which seem to him backward. Even in cases in which the author's command of facts was no more backward than his analytical apparatus, he would stress the former and under-rate, as it seems to me, the importance of the latter point... he seems to overstate the importance of the experimental, and to understate the importance of the theoretic side of their work.

Schumpeter has taken Mitchell to task for thinking theory to be of secondary importance. He emphatically states that Marshall's fame and influence is rightly due to the analytical tools he forged in his fifth book. Schumpeter has gone beyond this and stated that it is the fifth book of the Principles (and matter placed elsewhere in that treatise which really belongs in that book) which is immortal in the sense in which scientific achievement can be called immortal.

This establishes the point that Schumpeter was strongly for the theoretical foundations upon which experimental and empirical economics should be established. But is must be pointed that he envisioned economic theory as a dynamic and evolving analytical engine. Like Pigou, he has said that more hands could be attached to the engine of economic analysis of economic theory. Much more important, he has said that to avoid obsolescence of economic tools of analysis newer insights need to be continuously added in the light of new factual knowledge. Sharpening of the existing tools and forging of the new tools is essential according to him.

As much as Schumpeter has been for the theory, there were certain parts and tendencies he was extremely unhappy about. One of the features of the mainstream economic theory to which Schumpeter objected was its static nature. As it is pointed out at other places in this work, he greatly admired Walras and was willing to give him the crown, i.e., the great economist of all the time. Schumpeter (1989, pp. 166-67) explicitly states that Walras was the first economist who constructed a general equilibrium system but, unfortunately, it was static. Schumpeter wanted to remedy this lacuna.

I felt very strongly that this was wrong, and that there was a source of energy within the economic system which would itself disrupt any equilibrium that might be attained. If this is so, then there must be purely economic theory of economic change which does not merely rely on external factors propelling the economic system from one equilibrium to another. It is such a theory that I have tried to build and I believe now, as I believed then, that it contributes something to the understanding of the struggles and vicissitudes of the capitalist world and explains a number of phenomena, in particular the business cycle, more satisfactorily than it is possible to explain them by means of either the Walrasian or Marshallian apparatus.

This is a rare yet a very clear statement of Schumpeter acknowledging the motive force of his own contribution.

The persistence of economic analysis predicated on the basis of perfect competition by the classical and neoclassical economists was of a grave concern to Schumpeter. His strong objection to the theory and practice was of much serious depth than the usual one that the stringent conditions of perfect competition either do not exists or are not very likely to exist. The argument that perfect competition results in the optimum allocation of resources and maximum efficiency were simply arguments which were construed proofs by the classicists and neoclassicists according to Schumpeter. In this sense, he believes, such a theory is simply a house of cards, i.e., this means there is no substance to that is worth from the point of view of the theory and reality. Entrepreneur's chase for maximum profit, even if it does not occur under the conditions of perfect competition, could result in maximum productive performance. Consequently, dynamic and innovative imperfect competition could result in maximization of production. Schumpeter (1942, p. 76) has clearly expressed this.

But between realizing that hunting for a maximum profit and striving maximum productive performance are not necessarily incompatible, to proving that the former will necessarily—or in immense majority of cases—imply the latter there is a gulf much wider than the classics thought. And they never succeeded in bridging it. The modern student of their doctrines never ceases to wonder how it was possible for them to be satisfied with their arguments or to mistake these arguments for proofs; in the light of later analysis their theory was seen to be a house of cards whatever measure of truth may be in their vision.

As far as the neoclassicists are concerned, Schumpeter has selected Marshall and Wicksell as the representatives. They were chosen by Schumpeter because of the enormous influence they have exerted on the minds of younger economists during their formative years. According to Schumpeter, Marshall and Wicksell had to undertake extremely restrictive assumptions to prove the proposition that under perfect competition output is maximized. Besides, they also found so many exceptions to the general proposition which tends to make the whole exercise nothing more than a truism.

In Schumpeter's view, this faulty outcome is because of the following two reasons: (1) the entire analytical apparatus, the house of cards as Schumpeter calls it, rests on the shaky foundations of static equilibrium. Schumpeter is never tired of pointing out that the capitalist reality is first and last a dynamic process of change, and (2) in Schumpeter's view, Wicksell substituted much diluted proposition by stating that perfect competition tends to produce maximum satisfaction of wants. Wicksell substituted the maximum satisfaction of abstract psychological phenomenon of utility for a more concrete and measurable magnitude of production which is inadmissible to Schumpeter. In his view any reasonable society adapts to circumstances and the classical and neoclassical framework also can work under socialism. The implication of his argument is that the model of perfect competition looses its uniqueness in theory as a vision of a theorist who wants to analyze capitalistic reality. Schumpeter very pointedly states that in their efforts to salvage and rigorize the doctrine of perfect competition Marshall and Wicksell rendered it emaciated and barely alive.

Schumpeter's 1946 *Encyclopedia Britannica* article indicates that he has retained his views intact on the subject of competition and imperfect competition. Schumpeter (1989, p. 200) restates his views clearly.

> The proposition that monopolies will sell smaller quantities of products at higher prices than will firms in conditions of perfect competition is true only under the proviso that other things—cost structures in particular—be strictly equal, and therefore has but little practical importance. Almost without exception, large-scale concerns do alter the cost structure of their industry, by introducing new methods of production and in other ways that are beyond the reach of numerous competing concerns of medium size. Therefore it does not follow that their outputs are actually smaller and prices actually higher than would be the outputs and prices with methods within the reach of competitive business.

The following statement of Schumpeter in which he has emphatically stated that economic history would be his first choice if he was starting afresh. This statement comes as a surprise to some, but it should not, intimate and comprehensive study of his life's creation in economics is built with the bricks and mortar of economic history. And that is what he has tried to communicate in the statement he (1954, p. 12) made.

> I wish to state right now that if, starting my work afresh, I were told that I could study only one of the three but could have my choice, it would be economic history that I should choose.

Schumpeter has listed three reasons for such a choice on his part. These reasons are clearly stated but they also reveal the secret of his mind and heart. First, in his view, economics happens in time and in that sense the content of economics is essentially a unique process in historic time. Second, economic events are intermingled with the institutional parameters that are not exclusively economic and consequently such a study enables us to understand better interrelationship of social sciences. Third, in this author's view, most important to Schumpeter were the fundamental errors committed in economic analysis which were due more to the paucity of historical experience rather than due to any shortage of economist's equipment. Building a grand dynamic economic system such as the one in his *Theory of Economic Development* with the raw materials of economic history was the manifestation of a theorist's vision to him. Constructing superstructure of a theory on the foundations of a few abstract and a priori propositions was not his notion and scheme of theory building. Without even Schumpeter's saying it, if an economic historian looks for the raw materials of his theory of economic development, one will find that they were mostly taken from the economic history of Germany.

Schumpeter's (1964, pp. 10, 177) statement below concerning the role of statistical and historical facts indicates clearly that these facts are to be the building block of knowledge.

> Statistical and historical facts have, on the one hand, more important roles to play in the building of our knowledge of a phenomenon than to verify a theory drawn from other sources. They induce the theoretical work and determine its pattern... only detailed historic knowledge can definitely answer most of the questions of individual causation and mechanism...

Richard Swedeberg has, unfortunately, drawn a wrong conclusion and taken a wrong turn which is totally out of tune with and is unfair to Schumpeter. Because Schumpeter had wished to be an economic historian, Swedeberg has drawn the conclusion that Schumpeter wanted to assign the key role to economic history and a secondary role to the economic theory. This is totally un-Schumpeterian because in his review of Mitchell's book, as discussed above, he unmistakenly and emphatically stated significance of economic theory. To this criticism Swedeberg would probably reply by saying that the review of Mitchell's book was written in 1930 and it was after the publication of Keynes's *General Theory* Schumpeter changed his views. But that would not be right because Swedeberg has quoted only the initial part of Schumpeter's statement from his *History of Economic Analysis*. Had he continued and gone into what Schumpeter has called 'third ground' for making the initial statement he would have found that Schumpeter wanted to learn more economic history because he firmly believed that it is due to the lack of knowledge of economic history that fundamental errors were made in economic theory. This further fortifies the belief that Schumpeter has always thought of economic history as building blocks of economic theory. After two pages in his *History of Economic Analysis* there is an elaborate discussion of economic theory. In this section, Schumpeter distinguishes between economic theory and economic analysis. Concepts such as marginal productivity, multiplier, accelerator are called the tools which are employed in economic analysis. From historical and statistical facts a researcher finds common elements. This process of scientific investigation in Schumpeter's (1954, p. 16) view culminates into an analytical finale.

> And finally we discover these schemata are not independent but related, so that there is advantage in ascending to a still higher level of 'generalizing abstraction' on which we construct a composite instrument or engine or organon of economic analysis... which functions formally in the same way whatever the economic problem to which we may turn it.

This refutes Swedeberg's insinuation that to Schumpeter economic history became more important than economic theory. This does disservice to both. Schumpeter advocated the conjugation of economic history and theory to improve the caliber and keenness of economic analysis. In the further discussion Schumpeter has admitted that performance of economic theory has been below expectations but has not stated that economic history should be given primacy. He has elaborately discussed the hostility and biases against economic theory and theory in general and has ably defended theory including economic theory as underperforming as it is.

Schumpeter wrote his paper "The Creative Response in Economic History" in 1947, but root of the idea lies in his *Business Cycles*. Essentially the same thought is expressed by Schumpeter in *Business Cycles* (1939, 1954, p. 46) when he has stated that by response to a certain change he means only what may be termed passive adaptation, i.e., adaptation within the fundamental data of the system. But when adaptation consists in altering some of those data to the class of internal change that is what Schumpeter calls a creative response.

In his 1947 work, Schumpeter has elaborated on the concept and process of creative response in the sense of a deepening knowledge. Schumpeter's ability of sounding afresh and giving more in discussing the old subjects is unique. This essay is a flower of Schumpeter's mature genius. It is like a luminous well-finished diamond with many lighted sides from within. When one thinks that nothing new possibly could be dug up on a subject, Schumpeter has managed give us pleasant and delightful surprises. What Schumpeter (1989, p. 73) has characterized of a book of weight is equally true of this piece of work.

Yet every book of weight tells us something beyond what it has to say about its particular subject. It conveys necessarily a general message from author to readers about methods, horizons, aims and views, of which the treatment of the subject in hand is about an application or paradigma.

In Schumpeter's view the creative response has three essential and distinguishable characteristics. First, it is unique from the point of view of explanatory causation. It cannot be explained on the basis of pre-existing facts. Every creative response materializes through different human motivation and mechanism, the threads of which have to be disentangled from the complicated fabric of historical time. A creative response is not a ditto or a copy of the one that has occurred in the past. This characteristic of it necessitates a detailed investigation of each and every creative response. Second, each creative response transforms the economic and social situation for good. The 'creative' in creative response carries that connotation. It obliterates the undesirable elements of the past without leaving any bonding solution to aglue the new social and economic situation with what could have been had the creative response not been born. Third, the amplitude of a creative response in a group, its intensity and success or failure hinges on (1) quality of personnel available, (2) quality personnel available in a particular area, and (3) individual decisions, actions and patterns of behavior as a response to the initial challenge.

Every creative response, as far as its economic aspect is concerned, materializes and comes to fruition due to the striving of entrepreneurs. Therefore, study of entrepreneurship is inseparably linked to creative response. In Schumpeter's view, the following distinctions have to be carefully made. Entrepreneurship is different from routine management. Ownership in capitalism is not vested with an entrepreneur, leadership and not ownership is the pith of entrepreneurship. Entrepreneur is not necessarily an inventor. An entrepreneur might have done all the things such as routine management, ownership and invention but for practical and conceptual reasons the two must always be separated. The heart and soul of entrepreneurship consists in getting new things done the sequences of which represent the capitalistic reality.

Larger gains going to the entrepreneur are justified in capitalism according to Schumpeter because it is in most cases only one individual or a few individuals who are able to overcome the reticence and hurdles when they do the things that are beyond what is considered routine and conventional. Another important thought put forward by Schumpeter deals with the sociological origins of entrepreneurs in Germany. Strong message that is conveyed here is that German entrepreneurs have come from all stratas of the German society. The person who filled the function was an entrepreneur regardless of his social origins. This definitely indicates that, unlike feudalism, capitalism is a system that rewards a person for getting new things done.

In Schumpeter's view large entrepreneurial gains should not be considered in isolation and in an absolute way. They should be considered in the context of an economy as a whole and in relation to the losses incurred by the unsuccessful entrepreneurs and capitalists. These gains also cannot be considered as net sectorial gains because the success of an entrepreneur imposes losses on losers in that sector. Masses in general fare better in the process of innovation but the idea in the traditional theory that capital moves across the industries in search of alternative gains is false and is unpalatable to Schumpeter. In his view, the capital is destroyed. From the point of view of this study an illuminating remark is made by Schumpeter (1989, pp. 227-8).

> Cumulation of carefully analyzed historical cases is the best means of shedding light on these things, of supplying the theorist with strategic assumptions, and banishing slogans.

Schumpeter's suggestion throws light on two points. One, it supports our contention that to Schumpeter theory building has always to be based on tested cumulative knowledge of economic history. Two, emotional content ought to be filtered out of the consideration of entrepreneurial gains which could be supported by cool analysis.

In "Theoretical Problems of Economic Growth," Schumpeter has commented on the nature and scope of economic growth. To him economic growth is not an autonomous phenomenon, i.e., it cannot be analyzed solely in economic terms. Non-economic factors impinge on economic growth. It is because such multivarious factors are involved in it, no monolithic theory can adequately explain the entire growth process. Systematic and stepwise analysis of the operant factors in the growth process is required. Of the total factors involved, some enhance the growth of an economy whereas the others stunt or retard the growth process. In this growth process, which involves both growth-promoting and growth-retarding forces, economic theory becomes a handmaiden to an economic historian. In a matrix of circumstances and outcomes, economic theory is helpful in identification of the direction and tendency of causation that flows from circumstances to particular results.

In the last part of this work Schumpeter is uncharacteristically critical of Adam Smith, John S. Mill and Marshall. Since the growth theory of the above three is well known, there is no reason to illustrate it here. To Schumpeter, their theory is like a tree in which newer branches sequentially grow out of the older ones in a predetermined and predictable way. The element in their growth process which Schumpeter finds most unpalatable is the passive nature of responses to the stimuli, i.e., absence of the pivotal role of the entrepreneur. Through the automatic and impersonal forces of the market system, saving investment and capital formation occurs. In a way Schumpeter has found their theory lifeless because of the absence of role of an entrepreneur. That intense drama of innovation, credit creation, creative destruction and temporary monopolies, based solely on innovation, are absent.

As a theory, what Schumpeter has found most objectionable about the Smith-Mill-Marshall Theory is that is is devoid of historical content. Schumpeter (1989, p. 239) has forcefully denounced such a theorization.

> I entirely empathize with the historian's aversion, which I often observed from "theories" or "philosophies" of history that have been produced in a quantity ever since seventeenth century; they were, at best, premature attempts at exploiting inadequate historical information and, at worst, rank dilettantism, the products of preconceived ideas—of ideological fantasy even—rather than serious research.

In his 1949 article, "Economic Theory and Entrepreneurial History," Schumpeter is sarcastic and defiant. Otherwise in criticizing others, e.g., his review of Mitchell's book, Schumpeter is very polite and proper. But the following of his remarks (Hugh G. J. Aitken, p. 57) indicate that this aspect concerning the neglect of the role of entrepreneur has been brewing in his mind and it has just boiled up and overflowed.

> For some of us the problem of economic development is all but solved so soon as natural and social conditions and political measures are stated—the rest follows automatically, and if entrepreneurs have anything to do with what actually happens they are a sort of beast of prey withholding the fruits of technological advance from community and sabotaging progress in their own interest. It is

needless to point out that this attitude is very prevalent in this country and that any attempt to take another view is for many a modern economist stigmatized as apologetics.

In this author's view this really was the reason for Schumpeter's disappointment towards the end of his life. It might not be as much per se the success of Keynes and his *General Theory*. The mainstream account of capitalistic growth without the entrepreneur and effective consequences his actions and the passive and impersonal forces of perfect competition that Schumpeter could not dislodge from the sacred precincts of the static economic theory. Worst of all, neoclassical economic theory in Schumpeter's view has no basis in historical facts and statistics. Schumpeter must have thought he had done what the greatest economist of all the time, Walras, could not do, that is to create a grand magnificent dynamic design which was rooted in historical reality. This he must have thought went unrecognized and unappreciated. What was appreciated was in fragments and, sometimes, what he thought to be unimportant.

Another interesting aspect of John Mill and Alfred Marshall's growth theory that is highly objectionable to Schumpeter is their relating growth of countries to race. The following remarks of Schumpeter (1989, p. 234) need to be carefully interpreted.

It is however, interesting to note that prominent economists, especially English ones, have been in the habit of emphasizing race. Nobody thinks of J.S. Mill—the utilitarian radical!—and A. Marshall as "racialist." Yet the racial note is unmistakable in the general introduction to both their principles.

Upon Reading Appendix A of Marshall's *Principles of Economics*, it is clear that according to Marshall race was definitely one of the factors figuring predominantly in human history in general and in economic progress in particular. But in the interest of accuracy and completeness, it must be stated that along with race, Marshall also discusses the impact on economic progress of factors such as climate, religion and creative minorities. Racial factor as a reason for economic progressiveness intrudes too much in Marshall's discussion. He (1962, p. 615) has stated the following regarding England.

The natural gravity and intrepidity of stern races that had settled on the shores of England inclined them to embrace the doctrine of Reformation; and these reacted on their habits of life, and gave tone to their industry.

Marshall's following statement might not go well with the Germans and Schumpeter.

> In every country, but especially in Germany, much of what is brilliant and suggestive in economic practice and economic thought is of Jewish origin.

It must be recalled that time Marshall grew up and lived was the time when the sun never did set on the British Empire and Britannia ruled the waves. Moreover, biological and anthropological studies conducted at the time made scholars think in terms of race. Today, looking at the phenomenal success of Japan and some of the less developed countries both Mill and Marshall readily would have revised their views. Economic development can be successfully imitated and imitators can surpass their predecessors in the game. But Schumpeter is right in criticizing both Mill and Marshall for putting so much emphasis in economic development on race. But their serious offense, according to Schumpeter, is not thoroughly studying economic history to form generalization.

Schumpeter could not and would not forgive the English growth theorists for being so blatantly oblivious of the pivotal role played by the entrepreneur and his act of creative response that launched an immense event such as the age of capitalism. For example, around 1840s the great English contractor Brassey had railways and docks under construction simultaneously in five continents. British capital flowed out to finance these entrepreneurial ventures. J.L. and Barbara Hammond (1951, p. 273) have recorded this important fact.

> At one time Brassey, the great contractor, had railways and docks under construction in five continents, and half the capital subscribed for French railways before 1847 came from British pockets.

In Schumpeter's view, such is the stuff of which capitalism and economic growth is made. Building growth theory on the assumptions of passive response of entrepreneur to opportunity, instead of he successfully creating and molding it, and automatic perfect competition was unrealistic and unforgivable as far as Schumpeter was concerned. It is not out of lack of knowledge of these century-making events that Marshall failed to incorporate them in his theory, because he (Marshall) was an astute observer of the business world of his time and before, but it is his unwillingness to use it as raw material in creating a dynamic general equilibrium system is what Schumpeter finds so objectionable.

Marshall's discussion of economic progress is full of references to race. Schumpeter's irritation concerning this aspect can be sorted out in the following way. First, Marshall made sweeping generalizations without adequate substantiation. Nobody can deny the significant role played by the Jewish entrepreneurs in the economic progress of Germany but a statement like that does seem to exclude the non-Jewish Germans such as the Krupps, Benzes, Mercedes, Siemens and many more. It also should be pointed out that since the Jews were excluded from ownership of land and, consequently, farming, the only way left for them was to be traders, merchants, money lenders and bankers. That in itself does not prove that was the reason they did best of the jobs because the were excluded from something. Some of them did best of the job precisely because they were capable people. As entrepreneurs they respond creatively to a stimuli. If looked at from Schumpeter's point of view, it becomes entrepreneur and his creative response and the argument gets out of racial determination.

Second, Marshall's generalization are expressed as absolutes as far as the race factor is concerned. Collective behavior of a group could be time determined. And such behavior may not have anything to do with race. Following quotation form Kindleberger (1978, p. 188) throws light on this subject.

> The Germans impressed Mme. de Stael in 1810 as sluggish-poets and thinkers, musicians and metaphysicians. By 1910, says Lowie, they were the Yankees of Europe. The early retardation is commented on widely, and frequently given a numerical estimate.

The factor that changed the situation radically in Germany was the defeat of Prussia by Napoleon in 1806. This event had the direct effect on ending feudalism in the west and indirect in the east. Ending of feudal bonds unleashed the energies of the Germans. In 1820 Germany was fifty years behind in the machine age, but with the help of foreign ideas and foreign capital equipment it made up in twenty years an industrial lag of half a century. This shows that people can change. Abolition of feudalism triggered the chain events. Societies can be changed for the better regardless of race. Besides, it must not be forgotten that Schumpeter was in Japan and must have seen the unprecedented rapid transformation of Japan. Schumpeter has tried to explain the initiation and the process of economic development independently of race because he was conversant with the factors discussed above.

As far as the conjugation of economic history and theory is concerned, Kindleberger (1978, p. 241) is in agreement with Schumpeter with a passing and a strong conviction.

It is in the nature of man to evangelize, to urge others to behave as he does, and I am no exception. It is my considered opinion, as well as my passionate conviction, that economics needs history even more than history needs economics.

Given the aforementioned discussion, we can say quite firmly that Schumpeter would have been delighted to hear and read Kindleberger's above remark.

Sir John Hicks in his *Theory of Economic History* has stated and elaborated on the significance of economic history, but his drift is in a different direction as compared to Schumpeter. According to Hicks, economic history should be used to arrive at certain generalizations, uniformities and laws that could be quantitatively supported. Hicks has stated that the theory of demand is a kind of generalization to which normal tendency of buyers could be associated with but not peculiarities of a particular consumer. Theories, in his sense, should be statements of general tendencies supported by statistical material. Sir John (1969, p. 5) has expressed his views in the following way.

No one would dream of claiming that there was any particular one man, any single inventor or entrepreneur, without whose activity the English Industrial Revolution could not have occurred. Though there is a sense in which Industrial Revolution is an event, it is itself a statistical phenomenon; it is a general tendency to which theory is unmistakably relevant.

Schumpeter would have no objection to using statistics, but as he has criticized Adam Smith, Mill and Marshall for not giving the major emphasis on entrepreneur, creative destruction and creative response. In fact, instead of whipping out statistical generalizations, as Hicks has proposed, Schumpeter would a researcher have study in details the acts of innovation because in his view every case is unique. Entrepreneur's response to an opportunity could be adaptive or creative. if it is adaptive, there no dynamic impulse that is imparted to the economic system. But if and when the response is creative, it sets in motion the process of creative destruction. Since the destruction is creative, old ways of doing business will be replaced by superior ways and methods. Industrial revolution as statistical phenomenon is an after effect of entrepreneurial creative response. It is the surface outcome of the act of leadership, though not ownership, and of getting things done by an entrepreneur. In his Business Cycle Schumpeter has bemoaned such methods of study. A researched has to fish out and study the deeper underlying causes in Schumpeter's view.

146

Bibliography

Arrow, K. and Hahn F. (1971), *General Competitive Analysis*, Holden Day Inc., San Francisco.

Ayer, A.J. (1972), *Bertrand Russell*, The Chicago University Press, Chicago.

Barro, Robert (1979 pp. 54-63), "Second Thoughts on Keynesian Economics," *Papers and Proceedings of the American Economic Assn.*, vol. 69, no. 2.

Barry, Norman (1981), "Restating Liberal Order: Hayek's Philosophical Economics," included in *Twelve Contemporary Economists*, ed. Shackelton J. and Licksley G., Halsted Press, New York.

Becker, G. (1971), *Economic Theory*, Alfred A. Knof, New York.

Bohm-Bawerk, E. (1980), *Capital and Interest*, McMillan and Co, London.

Black, M (1967), Probability, *Encyclopedia of Philosophy*, vol. 6, ed. Paul Edwards, McMillan, London.

Blaugh, R. (1985), *Economic Theory in Retrospect*, Cambridge University Press, London.

Brainard, W.C. and Perry, G. (ed.) (1984), *Brookings Papers on Economic Activity 2*, Washington, D.C.

Braithwaite (1973), *Scientific Explanation*, Cambridge University Press.

Brown, M. (1966), *On The Theory and Measurement of Technological Change*, Cambridge University Press, London.

Buchanan, J. (1970), *The Public Finances*, Richard D. Irwin, Homewood, Illinois.

Burch, J. (1986), *Entrepreneurship*, John Wilely and Sons, New York.

Clower, R. ed. (1969), *Monetary Theory*, Penguin Books, Baltimore.

Drucker, P. (1985), *Innovations and Entrepreneurship: Principles and Practice*, Harper Row, New York.

Drucker, P. (1986), *The Frontiers of Management*, E. F. Dutton, York.

Economist (March 19, 1988).

Encyclopaedia Britannica (1988), Vol. 6.

Fisher, F.M. (1966), *The Identification Problem*, McGraw Hill, New York.

Fisher, I. (1977), *The Theory of Interest*, reprinted by Porcupine Press, Inc., Philadelphia.

Fleming, T. and Grottfried, P. (1988), *The Conservative Movement*, Twayne Publishers, Boston, MA.

Fortune (June 6, 1988).

Georgescu - Roegen, Nicholas (1971), *The Enrtopy Law and Economic Process*, Harvard University Press, Cambridge, Massachusetts.

Goodwin, R. (1965), "A Model of Cyclical Growth," included in *Readings in Business Cycles,* ed. R. A. Godon and L. R. Klein, Richard D. Irwin, Homewood.

Haberler, G. (1951), "Schumpeter's Theory of Interest," *Review of Economics and Statistics,* 33:122-128.

Hahn, F. (1983), *Money and Inflation,* MIT Press, Cambridge, MA.

Hamiton, E. (1961), *Plato: Collected Dialogue,* Princeton University Press, Princeton, N.J. Bollingen Series LXXI.

Hammond, J. and Hammond, Barbara (1951), Eighth Edition, *The Rise of Modern Industry,* Methuen and Co. Ltd., London.

Hayek. F. (1967), *Prices and Production,* Augustus M. Kelley. Reprints in Economic Classics, New York.

Hicks, J.R. (1969), The Theory of Economic History, Clarendon Press, New York.

Hicks, J.R. (1983), *The Classics and Moderns,* Harvard University Press, Cambridge, Massachusets.

Hicks, J.R. (1979), *Causality in Economics,* Basic Books, New York.

Harcourt, G. ed. (1985), *Keynes and His Contemporaries,* St. Martin's Press, New York.

Harrod, R. (1951), *The Life of John Maynard Keynes,* Norton and Company, New York.

Harrod, R. (1967), "Increasing Returns," included in *Monopolistic Competition Theory: Studies in Impact,* ed. R. E. Kuenne, John Wiley and Sons, New York.

Hume, D., "Of Money," included in *Source Readings in Economic Thought,* ed. P. C. Newman, A.D. Gayer and M. H. Spencer.

Hutchison, T. (1980), *The Limitations of General Theories in Macroeconomics,* American Enterprise Institute, Washington, D.C.

Huxley, A. (1937), *Ends and Means,* Chatto and Windus, London.

Kaldor, N. (1952), "Market Imperfections and Excess Capacity," *Readings in Price Theory,* ed. G. J. Stigler and K. E. Boulding, Richard D. Irwin, Chicago.

Kalecki, M. (1954), *The Theory of Economic Dynamics,* Allen and Unwin, London.

Keynes, J. (1921, 1973), *A Treatise On Probability,* St. Martin's Press, New York.

Keynes, J. (1931, 1963), *Essays in Persuasion,* W.W. Norton and Company, New York.

Keynes, J. (1936), *The General Theory of Employment, Interest and Money,* Harcourt Brace, New York.

Keynes, J. (1971), *A Treatise on Money. The Pure Theory of Money,* Vol. 1, Macmillan, London.

Keynes, J. (1971), *A Treatise on Money. The Applied Theory of Money*, Vol. 2, Macmillan, London.

Keynes, J. (1973), *General Theory and After*, Collected Writings of John Maynard Keynes, Vol. XIII, ed. Donald Moggridge, Part I Preperation, Macmillan, London.

Kindleberger, C.P. (1978), *Economic Response*, Harvard University Press, Cambridge, Massachusetts.

Klein, L.R. (1965), *An Introduction to Econometrics*, Prentice Hall, Englewood Cliffs, New Jersey.

Knight, F. (1921, 1965), *Risk, Uncertainty and Profit*, Harper and Row Publishers, New York.

Kruger, L., Gigerenzer, G., and Morgan, M. (ed.) (1989), *Probabilistic Revolution*, Vol. 2, A Bradford Book, Sciences, Second Printing, Cambridge, Massachusetts.

Kuznets, S. (1974), *Population, Capital and Growth*, Norton and Company, New York.

Labich, K., (June 6, 1988), "The Innovators," *Fortune*.

Landau, R. (June 1988), "U.S. Economic Growth," *Scientific American*, Vol. 258, no. 6.

Letwin, W. ed. (1972), *A Documentary History of American Economic Policy Since 1789*, W.W. Norton and Company, New York.

Lewis, A. (1955, 1970), *The Theory of Economic Growth*, Harper and Row, New York.

Linder, S. (1970), *The Harried Leisure Class*, Columbia University Press, New York.

Lucas, R. Jr. (1975), "An Equilibrium Model of The Business Cycles," *Journal of Political Economy*, Vol. 83, No. 6, pp. 1113-1114.

Maddison, A. (June 1987), "Growth and Slowdown in Advanced Capitalist Economics," *Journal of Economic Literature*, Vol. XXV no. 2.

Mann, T. (1980), *Buddenbrooks*, Alfred A. Knoff, New York.

Marshall, A. (1919, 1923), *Industry and Trade*, Reprints of Economic Classics, Augustus M. Kelley, New York, 1970.

Marshall, A. (1962), *Principles of Economics*, English Language Book Society and Macmillan and Co. Ltd., London.

Matthews, R. (1959), *The Business Cycle*, Cambridge University Press, London.

Menard, Claude (1987), *The Probability Revolution*, vol. 2, ed. L. Kruger, G. Gigenrenzer and M. Morgan, Cambridge, Massachusetts.

Metzler, L. (1966), "Wealth Saving and Rate of Interest," included in *Monetary Theory and Policy*, ed. Richard S. Thorn, Random House, New York.

Muth, J. (1968), "Rational Expectations and the Theory of Price Movements," included in *Economic, Stastics and Econometrics*, ed. Arnold Zellner, Little Brown and Company, Boston, 1968.

Myint. H. (1948, 1965), *Theories of Welfare Economics*, Augustus M. Kelley, Reprints of Economic Classics, New York.

Nurkse, R. (1953), *Problems of Capital Formation in Underdeveloped Countries*, Oxford University Press, New York.

Okun, A. (1983), *Economics for Policy Making, Selected Essays of Arthur M. Okun*, edited by Joseph A. Pechman, MIT Press, Cambridge Massachusetts.

Pinson, K. (1966), *Modern Germany*, The Macmilan Company, New York.

Rostow, W. (1952), *The Process of Economic Growth*, Norton and Company, New York.

Russell, B. (1967), *The Autobiography of Bertrand Russell, 1872-1914*, An Atlantic Monthly Press Book, Little Brown and Company, Boston.

Russell, B. (1959), *Problems of Philosophy*, A Galaxy Book, Oxford University Press, New York.

Russell, B. (1948), *Human Knowledge: Its Scope and Limits*, Fourth Printing, Simon and Schuster, New York.

Ruttan, V. (1971), "Usher and Schumpeter on Invention, Innovation and Technological Change, included in *Economics of Technological Change*, ed. Nathan Rosenberg, Penguin Books, Baltimore.

Samuelson, P. (1943, 1966), *Collected Scientific Papers of Paul A. Samuelson*, ed. J. E. Stiglitz, MIT Press, Cambridge, MA.

Sargent, T. (1979), *Macroeconomic Theory*, Academic Press, New York.

Schumpeter, J. (1989), *Essays, Entrepreneurship, Innovations Business Cycles and Evolution of Capitalism*, (ed.) Richard V. Clemence, Transactions Publishers, New Brunswick (U.S.A.).

Schumpeter, J. (1911, 1934, 1961), *The Theory of Economic Development*, Oxford University Press, New York.

Schumpeter, J. (1939, 1964), *Business Cyles*, abridged in 1964 by Rending Fels. McGraw-Hill, New York.

Schumpeter, J. (1949), "Economic Theory and Entrepreneurial History," included in *Explorations in Enterprise*, ed. Hugh G.J. Aitken, Harvard University Press, Cambridge, MA.

Schumpeter, J. (1951, 1965), *Ten Great Economists*, Oxford University Press, New York.

Schumpeter, J. (1954), *History of Economic Analysis*, Oxford University Press, New York.

Scitovsky, Tibor (1976), *The Joyless Economy*, Oxford University Press, New York.

Smith, A. (1937), *The Wealth of Nations*, ed. Edwin Cannon, Random House, New York.

Smithies, A. (1965), "Economic Fluctuations and Growth", ed. R. A. Gordom and L. R. Klein, Richard D. Irwin, Homewood.

Solow, R. (1965), *Capital Theory and Rate Return*, Rand McNally and Company, Chicago.

Sraffa, P. (1952), "The Laws of Returns Under Competitive Conditions," included in *Readings in Price and Theory*, ed. G. J. Stigler and K. E. Boulding. Richard D. Irvin, Chicago.

Stein, H. (1969), *The Fiscal Revolution in America*, Chicago University Press, Chicago.

Stigler, G. (1965), *Essays in History of Economics*, University of Chicago press, Chicago.

Surrey, M. (1988), "Keynesian Economics," included in *J.M. Keynes in Retrospect*, ed. John Hillard, Aldershot, Hants, England: E. Elgar.

Tobin, J. (1982), *Essays in Economics: Theory and Policy*, The MIT Press, London.

Tobin, J. (1987), *Policies for Prosperity, Essays In Keynesian Mode*, (ed.) P.M. Jackson, MIT Press, Cambridge, Massachusetts.

The Wall Street Journal (Friday, May 13, 1988)

The World Bank (1983), Development Report.